THE GREAT CHRISTIAN LIE

THE GREAT CHRISTIAN LIE
The Truth on Passion Week

by
JACK C. DESELMS

THE GREAT CHRISTIAN LIE

Copyright © 2017 by Jack C. DeSelms

All rights reserved. No part of this book may be reproduced in any form or by any means—whether electronic, digital, mechanical, or otherwise—without permission in writing from the publisher, except by a reviewer, who may quote brief passages in a review.

World Ahead Press is a division of WND Books. The views and opinions expressed in this book are those of the author and do not necessarily reflect the official policy or position or WND Books.

Scripture taken from the New King James Version®. Copyright © 1982 by Thomas Nelson. Used by permission. All rights reserved.
Scripture taken from King James Version (KJV) is Public Domain

Paperback ISBN: 978-1-9442112-76-6
eBook ISBN: 978-1-944212-77-3

Printed in the United States of America
16 17 18 19 20 21 LSI 9 8 7 6 5 4 3 2 1

CONTENTS

	Introduction	7
1.	First Fruits	13
2.	Not Friday	17
3.	Prior to Passion Week	19
4.	Friday and Saturday – Before Passion Week	22
5.	Palm Sunday	24
6.	Sunday Night	29
7.	Monday Daytime, Eleventh of Nisan	32
8.	Olivet Discourse: Monday Night	41
9.	Passover Comments	50
10.	Tuesday Daytime, Twelfth of Nisan	56
11.	The Last Supper	58
12.	Jesus and the Disciples go to Gethsemane	70
13.	Garden of Gethsemane	77
14.	Jewish Judicial Procedure Violated	81
15.	First Trial of Jesus – Annas: Tuesday Night to Dawn Wednesday, the Thirteenth of Nisan	83
16.	Second Trial – Caiaphas and Some of the Sanhedrin: Tuesday Night to Dawn Wednesday, the Thirteenth of Nisan	85

17. Third Trial – Caiaphas and the Full Sanhedrin:
    Wednesday Daytime, the Thirteenth of Nisan 88

18. Fourth Trial – Pontius Pilate First: Wednesday
    Daytime, the Thirteenth of Nisan 91

19. Fifth Trial – Herod Antipas: Wednesday Daytime,
    the Thirteenth of Nisan 93

20. Sixth Trial – Pontius Pilate Second: Wednesday
    Daytime, the Thirteenth of Nisan 94

21. Journey to Golgotha: Wednesday Daytime, the
    Thirteenth of Nisan 102

22. Jesus on the Cross: Wednesday Daytime, the
    Thirteenth of Nisan 105

23. The Crucifixion from A Scientific Standpoint 110

24. Signs at Jesus' Death: Wednesday Daytime, the
    Thirteenth of Nisan 115

25. Pilate Orders a Guard Set: Wednesday Night
    to Dawn Thursday, the Fourteenth of Nisan 119

26. Three Days and Three Nights: Saturday Night
    to Dawn Sunday, the Seventeenth of Nisan 122

27. Sunday Daytime, the Seventeenth of Nisan 127

28. The Road to Emmaus: Sunday Afternoon,
    the Seventeenth of Nisan 129

29. Jesus Appears to His Disciples: Sunday Night
    to Dawn Monday, the Eighteenth of Nisan 132

Bibliography 141

INTRODUCTION

The purpose of this book is to show that Jesus Christ was crucified on Wednesday and not on Friday. The idea that Jesus was crucified on Good Friday is a lie that has been promulgated and repeated so many times since it was codified by the Council of Nicaea in 325 AD, that it has become an indisputable fact. There was a deliberate effort by the Church of Rome to separate the event from the Biblical text. Some early Jerusalem Christians were called (Latin) Quartodecimans. They held to the belief that the crucifixion was done on the fourteenth of Nisan, Passover, three days after that the Resurrection took place. They were eventually ex-communicated from the church.

> *It appeared an unworthy thing that in the celebration of this most holy feast we should follow the practice of the Jews, who have impiously defiled their hands with enormous sin, and are, therefore, deservedly afflicted with blindness of soul [. . .] Let us then have nothing in common with the detestable Jewish crowd; for we have received from our Savior a different way.* [1]

Here is another example of early church anti-Semitism:

> *It was, in the first place, declared improper to follow the custom of the Jews in the celebration of this holy festival,*

> *because, their hands having been stained with crime, the minds of these wretched men are necessarily blinded. [. . .] Let us, therefore have nothing in common with the Jews, who are our adversaries. [. . .] avoiding all contact with that evil way. [. . .] who, after having compassed the death of the Lord, being out of their minds, are guided not by sound reason, but by an unrestrained passion, wherever their innate madness carries them. [. . .] a people so utterly depraved. Therefore, this irregularity must be corrected, in order that we may no more have anything in common with those parricides and the murderers of our Lord. [. . .] no single point in common with the perjury of the Jews.* [2]

The early church was insisting on moving the crucifixion from the fourteenth of Nisan to some other day. The Council of Nicaea, in 325 AD, agreed that all churches should celebrate Easter (the Resurrection) on the same day, but did not designate the date. Over time, various dates were used, and today Easter is celebrated on the first Sunday after the full moon following the Vernal Equinox. If the full moon occurred on a Sunday, and thereby coincide with the Passover, Easter was celebrated on the following Sunday. This deliberately ensured that Easter would never be celebrated on Passover.

From this, we can clearly see that the early church would do whatever was necessary to eliminate any Jewish influence on the Crucifixion and resurrection of Jesus. It is important to remember that Jesus was a Jew, followed Jewish customs, and obeyed Jewish law. When we remember this fact, and quit trying to apply Christianity to these events, the picture becomes clearer.

Easter

Name given by Anglo-Saxons to the Christian Passover as the Feast of Resurrection, and rather incorrectly used for the Jewish Passover (Acts xii. 4, A. V.). Originally "Pascha," or "Passover," was the name given by the Christians to the fourteenth day of Nisan as the day of the Crucifixion, corresponding to the eve of the Jewish Passover, the season of the sacrifice of the paschal lamb; this was followed by the memorial of the Resurrection on the succeeding Sunday; the former was regarded as a day of fasting and penitence, the latter as a festival of joy. Under the first fifteen bishops of Jerusalem, who were all Jews, no difference occurred between the Jewish and the Christian dates.

In the course of time it appears that custom and tradition differed in the various churches of the East and the West, some laying stress upon Friday as the historical day of the Crucifixion, others again adhering more to the Jewish custom of celebrating the fourteenth day of Nisan; but as the anti-Judean element obtained ascendency, the connection of the Jewish and the Christian Passover was severed, and adhesion to the fourteenth day of Nisan by Christians (the "Quatrodecimani") was condemned as heresy. Greater stress was laid, in the Western Church at least, on the connection of Easter with the vernal equinox of the sun than with the full moon of the fourteenth of Nisan. In other words, Easter became a solar date, whereas Passover was essentially lunar. The Metonic cycle was, however, employed by both Jews and Christians to reconcile the calculations by sun and moon respectively; Passover and Easter always occur, therefore, about the same time of the year, though they only rarely fall on the same day. At the Nicene Council in 325 it was decided that the Christian Passover should be celebrated on the Sunday following the full moon of the vernal equinox (March 21); and in the Western Church it was decreed that, in case the full moon falls on Sunday, so that there arises the possibility of a common celebration of Passover by Christians and Jews, the Christian Passover should be postponed until the next Sunday; the reason for this given by Emperor Constantine (Socrates, "Hist. Eccl." i. 9) was that "it seemed very unsuitable that we should follow this custom of the Jews, who, constantly erring in the utmost degree, celebrate the Feast of Passover a second time in the same year"; i.e., celebrate it sometimes before the spring equinox. [3]

With God's blessing and leading, we will discover the truth, and perhaps learn a few things about Jesus' time and teachings. I have included the events of that block of time as I have been led to understand them. This book has been written after much prayer, study, and contemplation. My task has been to be a scribe for the Author.

I have organized this section of the book into night and day blocks of time, in accordance with the Jewish method of tracking time. When considering a day, such as the eighth of Nisan, the night always precedes the day.

Psalm 22 and Isaiah 53

These two chapters provide a prophecy of the events. They accurately describe what is to happen. These two prophecies deserve close reading and introspection. I have selected a few verses to highlight:

INTRODUCTION

My God, My God, why have You forsaken me?
Why are You so far from helping Me,
And from the words of My Groaning (Ps. 22:1).

He trusted in the Lord, let Him Rescue Him;
Let Him deliver Him, since He delights in Him (Ps. 22:8)!

For dogs have surrounded Me;
The congregation of the wicked has enclosed Me.
They pierced My hands and My feet (Ps. 22:16).

They divide My garments among them,
And for My clothing they cast lots (Ps. 22:18).

But He was wounded for our transgressions,
He was bruised for our iniquities;
The chastisement for our peace was upon Him,
And by His stripes we are healed (Isa. 53:5).

The Great Christian Lie: The Truth on Passion Week

CHAPTER ONE

FIRST FRUITS

Seven is God's perfect number and when you see a group of seven (or multiples of seven), that is God's sign that this list is important to him.

The simplest way to anchor the Passion Week calendar is to set the ending date. The tomb was discovered to be empty on the first day of the week, the day we call Sunday. The Feast of First Fruits is established as the first day after the sabbath (Lev. 23:11). This is the day of new beginnings. Let us consider other examples of new beginnings.

One: Noah's Deliverance – Gen. 8:4

"Then the ark rested in the seventh month, the seventeenth day of the month, on the mountains of Ararat." Prior to the escape from Egypt, Nisan was the seventh month. On the seventeenth of Nisan, the world had its new beginning.

Two: Israel Moved to Egypt – Ex. 12:41

Jacob's family moved to Egypt to escape the famine in the Holy Land on the seventeenth of Nisan exactly 430 years before leaving Egypt. On the seventeenth of Nisan, Israel had its new beginning.

Three: Israel's Journey from Egypt – Num. 33:1–8

Please remember that Israel tracked time from sundown to sundown, that is the evening of a date comes before daytime. On the seventeenth of Nisan, Israel had its new beginning.

> *These are the journeys of the children of Israel, who went out of the land of Egypt by their armies under the hand of Moses and Aaron. Now Moses wrote down the starting points of their journeys at the command of the Lord. And these are their journeys according their starting points:*
>
> *They departed from Rameses in the first month* [Nisan is now the first month], *on the fifteenth day of the first month; on the day after the Passover* [still the fifteenth of Nisan] *the children of Israel went out with boldness in the sight of all the Egyptians. For the Egyptians were burying all their firstborn, whom the Lord had killed among them. Also on their gods the Lord had executed judgments.*
>
> *Then the children of Israel moved from Rameses and camped at Succoth* [evening of the fifteenth]. *They departed from Succoth and camped at Etham* [evening of the sixteenth], *which is on the edge of the wilderness. They moved from Etham and turned back to Pi Hahiroth, which is east of Baal Zephon; and they camped near Migdol* [evening of the seventeenth]. *They departed from before Hahiroth and passed through the midst of the sea into the wilderness* [morning of the seventeenth], *went three days' journey in the Wilderness of Etham, and camped at Marah.*

Four: Joshua Gets His Orders for the Battle of Jericho – Josh. 5:10–14

The Commander of the army (Jesus) then gave Joshua the instructions for conquering Jericho and the battle for control of Canaan began. On the seventeenth day of Nisan, Israel began its battle to conquer Canaan.

Now the children of Israel camped in Gilgal, and kept the Passover of the fourteenth day of the month [Nisan] *at twilight on the plains of Jericho. And they ate of the produce of the land on the day after the Passover* [the fifteenth of Nisan], *unleavened bread and parched grain, on the very same day. Then manna ceased on the day after* [the sixteenth of Nisan] *they had eaten the produce of the land; and the children of Israel no longer had manna, but they ate the food of the land of Canaan that year.*

And then it came to pass [the seventeenth of Nisan], *when Joshua was by Jericho, that he lifted his eyes and looked, and behold, a Man stood opposite him with His sword drawn in His hand. And Joshua went to Him and said to Him, "Are You for us or for our adversaries?" So He said, "No, but as Commander of the army of the Lord I have now come." And Joshua fell on his face to the earth and worshiped, and said to Him, "What does my lord say to His servant?"*

Five: Queen Esther Saves Israel – Est. 3:12

On the thirteenth of Nisan, at Herman's urging, King Ahasuerus decreed that all Jews were to be killed. In Esther 4:16, it is recorded that Queen Esther called for all of Israel to not eat or drink for three days. On the sixteenth, Queen Esther went to the king and requested that Haman and the king come to a banquet the following day. At the banquet the next day, Queen Esther exposed Harman's plot and he was hung. On the seventeenth day of Nisan, Israel was saved from extermination.

Six: King Hezekiah Cleans and Sanctifies the Temple – 2 Chron. 29:17

Prior to this the priests had cleaned the temple and removed the debris that was found throughout. "Now they began to sanctify on the first day of the first month [Nisan], and on the eight day of the month they came to vestibule of the Lord. So they sanctified the house of the Lord in eight days, and on the sixteenth day of the first month they finished." On the seventeenth of Nisan, Israel restored temple worship.

Seven: Jesus Rose From the Tomb – Mark 16:6

Jesus was the first fruit of our salvation and he was raised on the seventeenth of Nisan. From this we can establish that Sunday was the seventeenth of Nisan and resurrection Sunday.

CHAPTER TWO

NOT FRIDAY

There are several reasons that I discount that the crucifixion happened on Friday. The Biblical passages below highlight this rationale:

Jesus Travels to Bethany – John 12:1

Six days before Passover, Jesus and the disciples traveled to Bethany. The Passover could not have been on a Friday because that would have put Jesus traveling on the sabbath. The maximum distance to travel on a sabbath day was about one mile.

Pilate's courtyard – John 18:28

When the members of the Sanhedrin took Jesus before Pilate, they would not have entered Pilate's courtyard because they would have become defiled and would not be able to eat the Passover meal. The Passover meal was eaten after sundown on Wednesday and this had not yet happened.

Jesus Speaks about His Death and Resurrection – Matt. 12:40

Jesus said that he would be three days and three nights in the heart of the earth: Wednesday night, Thursday day, Thursday night, Friday day, Friday night, Saturday day.

The resurrection happened Saturday night, before dawn on Sunday.

Sabbath Translation – Matt. 28:1

"Now after the Sabbath" is a wrong translation. It should be "sabbaths", plural. The Greek word for "sabbath" that was used in the original Greek manuscripts was a plural noun. The Feast of Unleavened Bread was a high sabbath, and the seventh day (Saturday) was a sabbath.

CHAPTER THREE

PRIOR TO PASSION WEEK

Let us now review some of the activities that happened just before the Passion Week:

Jesus Resurrects Lazarus – John 11:1–45

Jesus received word from Mary and Martha that Lazarus had died, and he then waited two more days before setting out for Bethany. When he arrived, Lazarus had been in the grave four days. Jesus raised Lazarus from the dead and many believed that Jesus was the true Messiah. There was a Jewish superstition of that day that said a soul stayed near the grave for three days, hoping to return to the body. Therefore, it was accepted that after four days there was absolutely no hope of resuscitation. It is believed that Jesus waited so there would be no question about raising Lazarus from the dead and God was glorified by raising him.

Word of Lazarus's Resurrection Spreads – John 11:46–48

The Lazarus event was reported to Pharisees who were concerned that Jesus would cause such uproar among the Jews that the Romans would take away their position and nation.

Priests and Elders Discuss Jesus – John 11:49–50; Matt. 26:3; Mark 14:2; Luke22:2

The high priest (Caiaphas), past high priests, priests who were the heads of the twenty-four courses, senior priests who were destined for leadership positions, and elders met in Caiaphas' courtyard and discussed what to do about Jesus. They agreed to arrest and kill Jesus, but they were afraid that the people would riot and cause the Romans to quell the disturbance. The high priest Caiaphas said, "You know nothing at all, nor do you consider that it is expedient for us that one man should die for the people and not that the whole nation should perish" (John 11:49–50).

Caiaphas was appointed High Priest by the Roman Governor and he retained this position by keeping the Jews calm. That meant, of course, threats to the political stability of Jerusalem would need to be handled swiftly and efficiently. If the Roman's got involved, it was likely that many would be killed, and possibly the Temple destroyed. Jesus' followers were the unknown factor and the Jewish leaders did not want to get them upset. There was no concern about God getting upset.

Pharisee Involvement – John 11:53

The Pharisees from that point on plotted on how to kill Jesus.

Jesus Moves to Ephraim – John 11:54

Because of this threat, Jesus no longer walked openly among the Jews and retired to the city of Ephraim, about a day's journey from Bethany and Jerusalem.

Speculation – John 11:55–56

There was much speculation and rumor among the people about Jesus coming to Jerusalem for the Passover.

Jesus is Outlawed – John 11:57

The Chief Priest and the Pharisees gave the command that should anyone see Jesus, they were to report where he was that they might seize him.

There was much Jewish excitement that the Messiah would save Israel from Rome. Hayyin Schauss notes in his book, *Guide to Jewish Holy Days: History and Observance*, that the Jews believed that the soon coming Messiah was going to rescue them, much as Moses did.[1] The excitement grew to a fever pitch at Passover, which contributed to the fear that the church leaders felt when Jesus came into town and went to the temple. This sheds some light on the excitement surrounding the Triumphal Entry on Sunday, the tenth of Nisan.

CHAPTER FOUR

FRIDAY AND SATURDAY – BEFORE PASSION WEEK

Friday Daytime, the Eighth of Nisan – John 12:1

Six days before the Passover (the fourteenth of Nisan) Jesus and the disciples traveled from the city of Ephraim to Bethany and stayed with Mary, Martha, and Lazarus.

Friday Night to Dawn Saturday, the Ninth of Nisan

This was the Jewish weekly sabbath. Jesus and the disciples rested at Bethany with Mary, Martha, and Lazarus.

Saturday Daytime, the Ninth of Nisan

This was the Jewish weekly sabbath. Jesus and the disciples rested at Bethany with Mary, Martha, and Lazarus.

Saturday Night to Dawn Sunday, the Tenth of Nisan – John 12:2

Jesus and the disciples spent the remainder of the sabbath in Bethany and after sundown on Saturday, Martha prepared dinner for them.

Jesus is Anointed – John 12:3–8

John records that Mary anointed Jesus' feet with costly perfume and wiped them with her hair. Mary had a very valuable bottle of spikenard, a product of southern India, in a sealed bottle. The bottle would have been sealed to prevent evaporation, requiring the neck to be broken to get the perfume out. She broke open the bottle and poured the contents over Jesus' feet. The whole house was filled with the fragrance of the perfume. Similar events are spoken of in Matthew 26:7–13, and Mark 14:3–9. All of them have a very common theme and words; they are just in different homes in Bethany: Martha and Mary's home and Simon the Leper's home. John speaks of Mary pouring the perfume on Jesus' feet, where Matthew and Mark speak of a woman pouring the perfume on his head. I believe that this is two distinct events on Saturday and Sunday night. Psalms 133:2 describes pouring oil on the heads of kings and priests. I can see how pouring oil on someone's head or feet would be a sign of love and respect.

Crowds Form in Bethany – John 12:9–11

A very large crowd gathered in Bethany because the people wanted to see Jesus and Lazarus. The priests determined to also put Lazarus to death because Jesus had resurrected him. Lazarus was proof that Jesus had the ability to raise people from the dead, which only God could do. Many people were leaving Judaism and following Jesus which was very threatening to the Jewish leadership.

CHAPTER FIVE

PALM SUNDAY

Sunday Daytime, the Tenth of Nisan – Ex. 12:3

"Speak to all the congregation of Israel, saying: 'On the tenth of this month every man shall take for himself a lamb, according to the house of *his* father, a lamb for a household'" (Ex.12:3). This is day that the Passover lamb was selected, taken to the temple, and presented to the priests for inspection. The lamb had to be perfect and without blemish to be acceptable as a sacrifice. Jesus presented himself as the ultimate sacrificial Passover lamb.

Gabriel's Prophecy – Dan. 9:25

Daniel predicted the coming of the Messiah. This prophecy was given by the Angel Gabriel in 445 BC and recorded in Daniel 9:25:

> *Know therefore and understand,*
> *That from the going forth of the command*
> *To restore and build Jerusalem*
> *Until Messiah the Prince [king],*
> *There shall be seven weeks, and sixty-two weeks;*
> *The street shall be built again, and the wall,*
> *Even in troublous times.*

Measurable Time

"From the commandment [. . .] until Messiah [. . .]" is a specific length of time. This is sixty-nine weeks of years, or 173,880 days. This period of time ended on Sunday, the tenth of Nisan. This was taken from *The Coming Prince* by Sir Robert Anderson, originally published 1881 and recomputed and published by other authors.[1]

Triumphal Entry – Matt. 21:1–22, Mark 11:1–11, Luke 19:29–40, John 12:12–19

These verses describe the Triumphal Entry, or what we call "Palm Sunday". Jesus and the disciples left Bethany and traveled two miles to Jerusalem. When they came to Bethpage, which was in the outskirts of Jerusalem, Jesus sent two disciples into town to find an ass and a colt. Consider that the ass might refer to the burdensome rites and ceremonies of the Jewish Law and the colt referred to the wild and untamed Gentiles. Speculation is that Christ first rode the ass and then the colt to show that he was the transition from Jewish law to the Gentile world.

This fulfilled the prophecy in Zechariah 9:9, "Rejoice greatly, O Daughter Zion! Shout, O Daughter of Jerusalem! Behold, your King is coming to you; He *is* just and having salvation, Lowly and riding on a donkey, A colt, the foal of a donkey."

According to Wikipedia, Bethany and Bethpage were producers of figs, so there would be a ready supply of palm branches.[2] Waving the palm branches was known as a sign of joy and victory and Christ was being received as King of Israel. Waving the palm has been a sign throughout Jewish history as a symbol of joy and Leviticus 23:40 provides the instructions.

Also, at the end of the Maccabee revolt, the people celebrated by waving palm branches.

Jesus is Honored as Royalty – 2 Kings 9:13

When the disciples brought the ass and colt to Christ, the people put their outer garments on the animals for him to sit upon. Again, this is was customary way to honor royalty.

The Son of David – Matt. 1:1

By calling Jesus the Son of David, they were proclaiming him to be the Messiah.

Multitudes of people lined the route Jesus took and sang, "Hosanna to the Son of David".

The Cornerstone – Ps. 118:22

"The stone which the builders rejected has become the chief cornerstone", the builders refer to the Jewish leaders who rejected Jesus, who had become the chief cornerstone.

The Crowds Quote Psalms – Luke 19:40

"Blessed is he who comes in the name of the Lord" is a quote from Psalms 118:26. When the Pharisees heard this they became upset and told Jesus to rebuke his disciples. Jesus answered, "I tell you that if these should keep silent, the stones would immediately cry out."

Jesus Mourns Jerusalem's Future – Luke 19:42

As Jesus drew near to entering Jerusalem, he wept over it, "If you had known, even you, especially in this your day, the things *that make* for your peace! But now they are hidden from your eyes." Jesus knew the future of Jerusalem and how it was to be destroyed in 70 AD, and he cried. Israel rejected Jesus, and there would be a terrible price for them to pay. Over a million people would die during the destruction of Jerusalem and the survivors would be taken as slaves to Rome. Jesus also knew that the Pharisees would be blind to his true character until near the end of the Great Tribulation when they would finally accept him as the Messiah.

Jesus Chooses His Route – Luke 19:45

As Jesus entered Jerusalem, the entire city was talking about him. Great crowds followed him throughout his entrance into the city. If Jesus wanted to assume earthly power, he would have gone to the Tower of David and assumed command. But, instead, he went to the temple, as the lord and proprietor of it, to preach in it, and to purge it.

Jesus Clears the Temple – Matt. 21:12–13, Mark 11:15–19, Luke 19:45–48

Jesus went into the temple of God and drove out all those who bought and sold in the temple, and overturned the tables of the money changers and the seats of those who sold doves. Jesus said to them, "It is written, 'My house is a house of prayer', but you have made it a 'den of thieves'" (Luke 19:45–48). The verses that Jesus quotes are taken from Isaiah 56:7 and Jeremiah 7:11.

Jesus' Ministry During Passover – John 2:14–17

The clearing of the temple described in Luke 19:45–48 was Jesus' fourth Passover. In his first, he made a 'whip' out of some cords and drove the livestock merchants and money changers out of the temple (John 2: 14–17). The second Passover (John 5:1) and third Passover (John 6:4) are recorded to record the events and establish a timeline. Jesus' last Passover is at the end of his third year. There can be no doubt that Jesus' ministry was only three years long.

Jesus Heals – Matt. 21:14–17

After purging the Temple, Jesus then ministered to the blind and lame. All this time the people were still calling out "Hosanna to the Son of David", which made the priests and elders angry. They asked if Jesus could hear what they were saying. Jesus answered, "Yes. Have you never read, 'Out of the mouth of babes and nursing infants you have perfected praise'" (Matt. 21:16). Jesus was quoting Psalms 8:2. The priests and elders wanted to kill him, but could not because of the crowds. After visiting the temple, he returned to Bethany.

CHAPTER SIX

SUNDAY NIGHT

Sunday Night to Dawn Monday, the Eleventh of Nisan – Matt. 26:6–7, Mark 14:3–9

This was the second anointing. Apparently, Jesus and the disciples went from the temple to Simon the Leper's house in Bethany for dinner. There is some discussion in the commentaries about this event. This was the second occurrence of the nard. A woman came to Jesus with a sealed, alabaster flask filled with nard, which was a valuable product of southern India. The text says a box, but the Greek could also mean a bottle or vase. The container would have been sealed to prevent evaporation, requiring the neck to be broken to get the perfume out. She broke open the bottle and poured the contents over Jesus' head. Refer to Psalms 23:5 where it is said that "You anoint my head with oil", and Psalms 133:2 where it is said, "It is like the precious oil upon the head". Both of these verses use pouring oil (perfume) over the head as a sign of love. The whole house was filled with the fragrance of the perfume.

Similar events are spoken of in John 12:3–8. All of them have a very common theme and words; they are just in different homes in Bethany: Martha and Mary's home and Simon the Leper's home. John speaks of Mary pouring the perfume on Jesus' feet, while Matthew and Mark speak of a woman pouring the perfume on his head. I believe that these are two distinct events on Saturday and Sunday night. The disciples murmured among themselves about the extravagance of her display, but Judas spoke out and exposed his heart. Both Matthew and Mark concur that this occurred at Simon the Leper's House.

Judas Speaks Out Against the Anointing – Matt. 26:8–9, Mark 14:4–5, John 12:4–5

Judas, who was the keeper of the money, asked, "Why was this fragrant oil not sold for three hundred denarii [a denarii was a day's wages for an ordinary worker] and given to the poor" (John 12:4–5). John 12:6 says that Judas stole money from the group's money box and wanted the money for himself. Judas represents all those who follow Jesus only for what they can get from him, not for how they can serve him.

Jesus Defends the Woman– Matt. 26:10–13, Mark 14:6–9, John 12:7

Jesus said to leave the woman alone because she was preparing him for burial. Jesus said, "For the poor you have with you always, but Me you do not have always" (John 12:8). The woman will always be remembered for her act of pure love for Jesus. We can show our love for Jesus by using all our resources for the work of his Kingdom.

Judas Betrays Jesus – Matt. 26:14–16, Mark 14:10–11, Luke 22:3–6

Judas left the dinner in Bethany and went straight to Caiaphas's house in Jerusalem to make the offer to betray Jesus. The priests were delighted and they gave him thirty pieces of silver. This is what it would cost to purchase a servant or slave according to Exodus 21:32. Judas then began to watch for an opportunity to betray Jesus when there were no crowds present.

Zechariah 11:12–13 predicts thirty pieces of silver and that it would be cast unto the house of the Lord for the potter. After the betrayal, Judas tried to give the money back to the priests, but they refused to accept it. Judas threw the money on the floor then went out and hanged himself. The priests used the money to purchase a plot of land, the potter's field, to bury those without family.

CHAPTER SEVEN

MONDAY DAYTIME, ELEVENTH OF NISAN

The Fig Tree is Cursed – Matt. 21:18–22, Mark 11:12–14

The next morning Jesus and the disciples arose very early, before their host could prepare a breakfast, and left Bethany. They passed by a fig tree with leaves, but no figs. Because the tree was lush with leaves, it seemed reasonable for there to be fruit on the tree but there was none. Jesus was hungry, but when he found no fruit on the tree, he said, "Let no fruit grown on you ever again" and the tree died right then and there (Matt. 21:19).

The disciples questioned how the tree withered away so soon. Jesus responded with a lesson on prayer and faith. When you pray for something, and if you truly believe it will happen, it will happen.

John Gill's Exposition on Matthew 21:19 posits that the tree represented the Jews.[1] There were great expectations for them because of their profession of religion, great pretensions to holiness, and the advantages they enjoyed. There should have been fruit of righteousness. But Jesus found nothing but mere words, empty boasts, an outward show of religion, and an external profession. Christ rejected them and in a little time afterward, the kingdom of God, the gospel was taken away from them. Their temple, city, and nation was utterly destroyed.

Jesus' Authority is Questioned – Matt. 21:23–27, Mark 11:27–33; Luke 20:1–8

When Jesus and the disciples came to the temple and Jesus began to teach, the priests and elders challenged his authority to teach. Jesus asked them, "The baptism of John—where was it from? From heaven or from men" (Matt. 21:25). the priests and elders retired a short distance away and discussed this question. The priests and elders believed that if they said, "from heaven", then they would be admitting that John was sent by God to proclaim Jesus as the Messiah. If they answered "man", then they would have been declaring that John was a fraud; however, the crowd believed him to be a prophet, a man of God. If they said that John was a fraud, the people would have rebelled against the priests and possibly killed them. The priests answered saying that they did not know. Jesus then said, "Neither will I tell you by what authority I do these things" (Matt. 21:27).

Parable of the Two Sons – Matt. 21:28–32

Jesus told a parable of a certain man that had two sons. The man told his sons to go work in the field. One said no, but changed his mind and went. The other said yes, but did not go. Jesus asked, "Which of the two did the will of *his* father" (Matt. 21:31).

The elders said the first. Jesus responded with, "Assuredly, I say to you that tax collectors and harlots enter the kingdom of God before you. For John came to you in the way of righteousness, and you did not believe him; but tax collectors and harlots believed him; and when you saw *it*, you did not afterward relent and believe him" (Matt. 21:31–32).

The "certain man" represented God. The first son represented the people of the land, sinners, tax collectors, and harlots. The sinners were hard-hearted and rejected God. John's preaching brought them to God, and they were baptized. The second son represented the priests who seemingly accepted God, but then rejected Jesus and God's forgiveness.

The Parable of the Wicked Vinedressers – Matt. 21:33–46, Mark 12:1–12, Luke 20:9–19

Jesus told another parable where a landowner (God) owned a vineyard (Israel, Isa. 5:7) and leased it to vinedressers (the priests, Levites, and scribes who were entrusted with the care of the Jewish people). When it was harvest time, the landowner's servants (prophets and other representatives of God) went to the vinedressers to get them to harvest the grapes. The vinedressers beat one, killed one, and stoned another (God's prophets and judges were beaten, killed, and stoned). The landowner sent more, and they were treated the same. He then sent his son (Jesus) and the vinedressers killed him. Jesus asked the elders what the owner should do to the vinedressers. The elders, not understanding the parable said that the owner should destroy them.

Jesus asked, "Have you never read in the Scriptures: The stone which the builders rejected has become the chief cornerstone. This was the Lord's doing, and it is marvelous in our eyes" (Matt. 21:42). This was a direct quote from Psalms 118:22. Jesus then said, "Therefore I say to you, the kingdom of God will be taken from you and given to a nation [Gentiles and then to all the nations of the earth] bearing the fruits of it. And whoever falls on this stone will be broken [all who are offended by Christ will be injured or broken]; but on whomever it falls, it will grind him to powder" (Matthew 21:43–44). When Christ falls on them, they will be ground to powder as the Roman legions did in 70 AD. The elders understood that Jesus was talking of them and wanted to lay hands on him, but the crowds were too large.

Parable of the Wedding Feast – Matt. 22:1–14

Jesus shared another parable when he spoke of the wedding feast. "The kingdom of heaven is like a certain king [God] who arranged a marriage for his son [Jesus], and sent out his servants [disciples] to call those that were invited to the wedding [Israel]; but they were not willing to come" (Matt. 22:2–3). He sent out his servants again (seventy this time), but the guests still were not willing to come. Some of the king's servants were beaten and some killed, just as all of the disciples except John were killed. When the king heard about how his servants were being treated, he sent his army to kill those who had murdered his servants and burned down their town (destruction of Jerusalem and sends Israel into exile).

Then the king told his servants that the wedding was ready, but those invited (Jews) were not worthy. He told the servants to go out to the roads and invite all (gentiles) to the wedding and the wedding hall was packed with guests. The king noticed a guest that was not wearing wedding clothes and asked him how he got into the feast without proper attire; Gill suggests that this person was not righteous and did not belong in the wedding party. [2] The guest was speechless; again, Gill suggests that there will be pleas from the hypocrites, but no righteousness. [3] The king directed his servants to tie him up and throw him into the street, where " [. . .] there will be weeping and gnashing of teeth. For many are called, but few are chosen" (Matt 22:13–14) This represents God's ministers and pastors binding up the hypocrites as tare and casting them into the fire of God's judgment.

The Pharisees Ask About Taxes – Matt. 22:15–21, Mark 12:13–17, Luke 20:20–26

Some Pharisees and Herodians (members of Herod's household and servants answerable to Caesar) complimented Jesus as a true man and teacher of the way of God. They were trying to entangle Jesus with his words and ask if it was lawful for a Jew to pay taxes to Caesar. They were hoping to ensnare Jesus and accuse him of sedition or treason so that they would have cause to charge him before the governor. Jesus recognized their hypocrisy and asked them why they were testing him. He then asked for a Denarii coin which had a mark showing that it was a Roman coin. He held up the coin and asked whose image and inscription was on the coin. They responded that it was Caesar's image. Jesus said, "Render therefore to Caesar the things that are Caesar's, and to God the things that are God's" (Matt. 22:21).

Sadducees Question Resurrection – Matt. 22:23–33, Mark 12:18–27, Luke 20:27–40

The Sadducees continued the attack on Jesus by asking him a question on the resurrection. They did not believe that there was such a thing as the resurrection; they denied that there were angels and spirits, they believed that there was no future state, and that the soul died when the body died. Their question was, "Now there were with us seven brothers.

The first died after he had married, and having no offspring, left his wife to his brother. Likewise the second also, and the third, even to the seventh. Last of all the woman died also. Therefore, in the resurrection, whose wife of the seven will she be? For they all had her" (Matt. 22:25–28). Jesus responded saying, "You are mistaken, not knowing the Scriptures nor the power of God. For in the resurrection they neither marry nor are given in marriage, but are like angels of God in heaven" (Matt. 22:29–30). He continued, " [. . .] God is not the God of the dead, but of the living" (Matt. 22:31–32). Jesus was explaining that even though the body dies, the soul continues to live. This quieted the Sadducees and they did not question him again.

The Greatest Commandment – Matt. 22:34–40, Mark 12:28–31

One of the Pharisees, who was a lawyer (scribe) asked Jesus which is the great commandment in the law? Jesus responded, "And you shall love the Lord your God with all your heart, with all your soul, with all your mind, and with all your strength.' This *is* the first commandment. And the second, like *it, is* this: 'You shall love your neighbor as yourself.' There is no other commandment greater than these" (Mark 12:30–31). The scribe answered with, "Well *said,* Teacher. You have spoken the truth, for there is one God, and there is no other but He.[3] And to love Him with all the heart, with all the understanding, with all the soul, and with all the strength, and to love one's neighbor as oneself, is more than all the whole burnt offerings and sacrifices" (Mark 12:30–33). Jesus replied, "You are not far from the kingdom of God" (Mark 12:34). No asked Jesus more questioned; he had silenced the Herodians, Sadducees, scribes, and Pharisees.

Jesus Questions the Crowds – Matt. 22:41–46, Mark 12:35–37, Luke 20:41–44

"While the Pharisees were gathered together, Jesus asked them, saying, 'What do you think about the Christ? Whose Son is He'" (Matt. 22:41). The Pharisees answered that He was the son of David. Then Jesus replied, "How then does David in the Spirit call him 'Lord', saying: 'The Lord [God] said to my Lord [Jesus], Sit at My right hand [You have done your mission well], Till I make Your enemies Your Footstool [Ps. 110:1]'" (Matt. 22:43–44). Jesus continued, "If David then calls Him 'Lord', how is He his Son" (Matt. 22:45). No one was able to respond and they did not pose any more questions. The crowd enjoyed the exchange.

Jesus Condemns the Scribes and Pharisees – Matt. 23:1–36, Mark 12:38–40, Luke 20:45–47

While the scribes and Pharisees were still nearby, Jesus condemned them for most of Matthew 23. He spoke about how they loaded the people with burdens that they did not take themselves. They loved the best seat at the feasts, the best seats in the synagogues, greetings in the marketplaces, and to be called "rabbi".

The rabbis loved the outward showing of reverence, but inwardly they were hypocrites. In verse 33, Jesus called them "a brood of vipers". He also called them, "Blind guides, who strain out a gnat and swallow a camel" (Matt. 23:24). They would clean the outside of a cup, but the inside would be filthy (Matt. 23:25). They made show of a clean and pure spirit, but inside they were full of leprosy.

Seven times Jesus says, "Woe unto you Scribes and Pharisees, hypocrites[. . .]" He asks, "How can you escape the condemnation of hell" (Matt. 23:33). Jesus said that he would send prophets, wise men, and scribes (apostles). He told the scribes and Pharisees that they would kill some of these prophets, wise men, and scribes. Some examples include Stephen, James, the brother of John (who Herod killed), the other James (who was thrown headlong from the pinnacle of the temple), Simeon (who was crucified). In verse 34, Jesus also said that some of them would be scourged and persecuted from city to city (including John, Peter, Paul, and Barnabas). Finally, he said that all of these things would come to pass upon this generation (Matt. 23:36); this did in fact happen within thirty-eight years (70 AD).

The Widow's Mites – Mark 12:41–44, Luke 21:1–4

As Jesus was sitting opposite the treasury, he saw how much the rich put in. Then he saw a poor widow put in two mites (very small coins worth a fraction of a penny). Jesus called his disciples together and said that the rich gave a portion from their abundance, but the widow put in more than the rich because she gave her whole livelihood. The quantity of the donation is not as important as the heart of the person donating. God valued her donation more than the donations from the rich.

Jesus Laments Over Jerusalem – Matt. 23:37–39, Luke 13:3–35

"O Jerusalem, Jerusalem, the one who kills the prophets and stones those who are sent to her! How often I wanted to gather your children together, as a hen gathers her chicks under her wings [to protect them], *but you were not willing! See! Your house is left to you desolate* [predicting the destruction of Jerusalem in 70 AD]; *for I say to*

you, you shall see Me no more till you say, 'Blessed is He who comes in the name of the Lord [which will bring to an end the Great Tribulation and Christ returns]'" (Matt. 23:37–39).

Jesus wished that Jerusalem would repent and accept him as Messiah, but they would not. The judgment is the destruction of Israel, and Jesus' absence until his Second Coming.

Jesus Predicts the Destruction of the Temple – Matt. 24:1–2, Mark 13:1–2, Luke 21:5–6

As they were leaving the Temple, his disciples came to him and wondered at the beauty of the temple. This was the last time Jesus was ever in the temple. The temple was known throughout the Roman Empire as a magnificent building. The Jews took it to be a symbol of God's glory that was invincible. It had been under construction for over forty years and the construction would continue into the late '60s AD. Jesus said that it would be utterly destroyed, "not one stone shall be left" (Matt. 24:2).

CHAPTER EIGHT

OLIVET DISCOURSE: MONDAY NIGHT

Signs of the End – Matt. 24:3–8, Mark 13:3–9, Luke 21:7–11

When Jesus and the disciples got to the Mount of Olives, Peter, James, John, and Andrew asked him privately, "Tell us, when will these things be? And what *will be* the sign when all these things will be fulfilled" (Mark 13:4). Very interestingly, the first thing Jesus said was a caution the disciples, "Take heed that no one deceives you. For many will come in My name, saying, 'I am the Christ,' and will deceive many" (Matt. 24:4–5). There were several who professed to be the messiah during the forty years after Jesus' crucifixion. They all were hunted down and executed by the Roman Army.

Jesus continued, "You will hear of wars and rumors of war. See that you are not troubled; for all these things must come to pass, but the end [of Jerusalem] is not yet" (Matt. 24:6). There were several insurrections during this same period, and all were met by the Roman army and tens of thousands were killed. Jesus continued, "For nation will rise against nation, and kingdom against kingdom. And there will be famines, pestilences, and earthquakes in various places. All these *are* the beginning of sorrows" (Matt. 24:7–8). These were signs of the real tribulation that was to come in 70 AD, which was a time where there were extreme sorrows. Sorrows also refer to a woman in travail (great birth labors).

Future Persecution and Evangelism – Matt. 24:9–14, Mark 13:9–13, Luke 21:12–19

> *"Then they* [the persecuting Jews] *will take you up to tribulation* [Sanhedrin] *and kill you* [all the disciples except John were martyred], *and you will be hated by all nations for My name's sake. And then many will be offended, will betray one another, and will hate one another. Then many false prophets will rise up and deceive many.*
>
> *And because lawlessness will abound, the love of many will grow cold* [persecution from Rome and Jerusalem]. *But he who endures to the end shall be saved. And this gospel of the kingdom will be preached in all the* [Gentile] *world as a witness to all nations, and then the end will finally come"* (Matt. 24:9–14).

More Signs of the End – Matt. 24:15–22, Mark 13:14–20, Luke 21:20–24

Matthew and Mark use the phrase "abomination of desolation", and Luke talks about Jerusalem being "compassed" with armies. The general belief is that they are all talking about the same event: Titus Vespasian's siege from 66 AD to 70 AD. The Webster Ninth Collegiate Dictionary defines "desolation" as a "barren wasteland".[1] The Roman Armies desolated areas as they conquered. What they could use, they took, what they couldn't use they destroyed. To the Jews, they were an abomination; not only because they consisted of heathen and uncircumcised men, but chiefly because of the images of their gods, which were upon their ensigns. Images and idols were always an abomination to the Jews. When the army entered the temple, they carried their ensigns with them, and defiled it. They also spilled the priest's blood in the temple when the Romans killed the Jews in the temple.

At the beginning of the siege, those who had read and understood the prophecy left Jerusalem immediately and went to the mountains. They were instructed not to re-enter their homes, leave their fields, and escape immediately. It would have been especially difficult if they were to run on the sabbath, or if they had newborn infants. But they had to run for their lives. Josephus writes that "never did any city suffer such miseries, nor did any age ever breed a generation more fruitful in wickedness than this was". [2] The Roman Army ploughed the temple area up, eliminating all evidence that it ever existed. The siege killed over a million Jews and many others were carried off as slaves to Egypt's mines. The strongest were taken to Rome and built the Coliseum that still stands today.

In 132 AD, Emperor Hadrian renamed Israel 'Phillistia' (Palestine), and built a city on top of what was left of Jerusalem, naming it 'Aelia Capitolina'. They built a pagan temple over the spot where the temple was, and offered sacrifices. In 135 AD another Jewish revolt was put down and about 580,000 Jews were killed.

More Warnings – Matt. 24:23–28, Mark 13:21–23

Jesus continued to warn the disciples that there would be many false christs and prophets. The disciples were warned not to believe them. Following the destruction of Jerusalem, many said that they were the Christ, and they were put down by the Roman Army. The country was in great turmoil following the destruction of Jerusalem.

Matthew finishes this section saying that, "wherever the carcass is, there the eagles [vultures] will be gather together" (Matt. 24:28). When will Jesus return? The same day the vultures gather around the corpses of the wicked slain in judgment. This will be after the battle of Armageddon. Mark finishes this section with Jesus telling the disciples to "[. . .] take heed; see, I have told you all these things beforehand" (Mark 13:23). Luke finishes this section with the prophecy, "[. . .] And Jerusalem will be trampled by Gentiles until the times of the Gentiles are fulfilled" (Luke 21:24).

Coming of the Son of Man – Matt. 24:27–28, Mark 13:24–27, Luke 21:25–28

When the Son of Man does return, everyone will know. It will be like a lightning bolt that starts in the east and goes all across the sky to the west (Matt. 24:27); there will be no doubt that Jesus has returned. I lived in Phoenix for a time and saw such a lightning bolt. It started on one horizon and continued to the other horizon and lit up the entire sky; the thunder rolled on and on. I didn't think that it would ever end. The buildings shook, the trees shook, and the very ground shook. It was awesome, as will be the returning of Christ.

Jesus Warns of Jerusalem's Destruction – Matt. 24:29–31

"Immediately after the tribulation of those days [. . .]", (Matt. 24:29) does not refer to some day in the future. Rather it refers to the period immediately after the destruction of Jerusalem in 70 AD. Matthew 24:34 says that this generation will not pass away until all these things have happened. From the time Jesus said this to the time of Jerusalem's destruction was thirty-eight years, one generation. The sun was not darkened literally, but rather the Shekina, or the divine presence in the temple, was eliminated with the destruction of the temple. The moon governed the Jewish calendar and all of the festivals, which came to an end with the destruction. The stars (which referred to religious leaders in parts of the Old Testament) were described as falling from heaven; this meant losing relevance and being put to shame, the powers of heaven shaken. With the destruction of the temple, the religious and governmental bodies were killed, disbanded, and/or taken as slaves. Other commentaries explain this refers to the end of times, and the actual return of Jesus. Both explanations fit the verses, so both are presented.

Lesson from the Fig Tree – Matt. 24:32–35, Mark 13:28–31, Luke 21:29–33

Jesus told the disciples a parable about the fig tree. He said that when the tree limbs are tender and put forth their leaves, summer is near. When you see the signs that are discussed, you know that the end is near. In Matthew 24:24, Jesus said that this generation would not pass away until all these things took place. Jesus closed with, "Heaven and earth will pass away, but My words will by no means pass away" (Matt. 24:35). All three gospels are almost verbatim, and leave very little room for alternative discussions.

Unknown Day and Hour – Matt. 24:36–44, Mark 13:32–37, Luke 21:34–36

Jesus said that no one knows when that day or hour will come, not the angels, not the Son, but only the Father. As it was in Noah's time, so it will be in the end time; people will be eating, drinking, marrying, living life because they were not aware.

Consider the Jewish wedding, the groom goes away to prepare a place for the bride, she waits for his return but does not know when it will be. The groom comes at a time known only to him. Jesus continued, "Then two *men* will be in the field: one will be taken and the other left.

Two *women will be* grinding at the mill: one will be taken and the other left" (Matt. 24:40–41). "But know this, that if the master of the house had known what hour the thief would come, he would have watched and not allowed his house to be broken into. Therefore you also be ready, for the Son of Man is coming at an hour you do not expect" (Matt. 24:43–44).

The Faithful or the Wicked Servant – Matt 24:45–51

Jesus asked, "Who then is a faithful and wise servant, whom his master made ruler over his household, to give them food in due season" (Matt. 24:45). This especially applies to pastors and ministers, but also applies to all of us whom Jesus has given a task or responsibility. How blessed will the overseer be when the master returns and finds that he has been taking care of the assigned tasks and responsibilities? But if Jesus' servant abuses his authority, behaves unfaithfully, is overbearing, and abuses trust in the church, he will be held accountable. The master will severely punish them, and send him to a place for unfaithful people. Much will be required from everyone to whom much has been given. Even more will be demanded from the one to whom much has been entrusted. Those that have accepted the responsibility of being a shepherd of God's flock will be held to a much higher standard in God's court. Those that are not faithful shepherds will be dealt with most severely.

The Ten Bridesmaids (Virgins) – Matt. 25:1–13

Jesus told another parable about the ten bridesmaids. The bridesmaids were to meet the arriving bridegroom with their lamps lit. Five were wise and kept oil for their lamps. The foolish five did not have enough oil, ran out, and tried to borrow from the five wise ones. When the groom arrives unexpectedly, those without oil were locked out of the wedding, and he said, "Assuredly, I say to you, I do not know you" (Matt. 25:12). Jesus closed with a warning to always be prepared because no one knows the hour the Son of man is coming.

According to Gill, in Matthew 25:1, the virgins represent the followers of Christ and the groom is Christ. The lamps refer to the gospel, and those with oil (Holy Spirit in their heart) are shining their light and spreading the gospel. Those without oil (Holy Spirit) do have light and will be locked out of the wedding.[3]

The Talents – Matt. 25:14–30

Jesus told another parable about the master who went on a trip. Before he left, he gave his servants talents. A talent is about the wages for a servant for a lifetime. He gave one servant five talents, the next two, and finally the last received one. This distribution was based on their ability. The servant, who received five, invested wisely and earned another five. The servant, who received two, invested wisely and earned another two. The third servant hid the talent and earned nothing. When the master returned, he settled accounts with the three servants. The first and second were rewarded by being put in charge of a large amount.

The third, who buried the money, told the master that he knew that the master was a hard man, harvesting what he did not plant and gathering where he had not seeded. The master called him an evil and lazy servant for not investing the money with the bankers and receiving interest. The master took the talent from him and gave it to the one who had ten and threw this one into the street where there will be weeping and gnashing of teeth. The third represents sinners who typically view God as hard, cruel, and unjust. Jesus gave us all gifts, abilities, and the gospel to share. We all did not receive the same gifts, but we all received some. God will hold us accountable for the abilities he gave each of us and whether we used them to forward the spread of the Gospel.

The Judgment of Nations – Matt. 25:34–46

Jesus talked about the judgment, sometimes also called "separating the sheep from the goats". He said that when the Son of man comes in his glory and all the angels are with him, he will sit on his throne. All of the nations (all individuals that have professed the Christian religion in all the nations of the world) will be assembled in front of him, and he will sort them out, like a shepherd separates the sheep from the goats. Those nations (the sheep) that fed the hungry also fed him; those that gave drink to the thirsty also gave him drink. Those that gave clothing to the needy, gave clothing to him. Those that have used their skills and were industrious, diligent, faithful, and laborious servants will be included as part of the sheep. The goats will be those nations (individuals) that did not take care of the needy. The goats will also include the hypocrites who were wicked, slothful, and unprofitable, many of whom now pass undistinguished and undiscovered. The sheep nations will go into eternal life and the goat nations will go into everlasting punishment.

Jesus Announces His Death – Matt. 26:1–2

Jesus then said to the disciples, "You know that after two days is the Passover, and the Son of Man will be delivered up to be crucified" (Matt. 26:2). Passover starts Wednesday at sundown, and the Son of man will be handed over to be crucified. Jesus is fulfilling his mission. Please note that Jesus said that he would be handed over to be crucified *after* two days, Wednesday. This establishes the date as Monday, the eleventh of Nisan.

Monday Night to Dawn Tuesday, the Twelfth of Nisan

No further events are listed for Monday night. After what Jesus went through in the Temple during the day, and his teaching on the Mount of Olives, it is plausible that he may have retired to Bethany and rested.

CHAPTER NINE

PASSOVER COMMENTS

Now the Lord spoke to Moses and Aaron in the land of Egypt, saying, "This month shall be your beginning of months [1 – Nisan]; it shall be the first month of the year to you. Speak to all the congregation of Israel, saying: 'On the tenth of this month every man shall take for himself a lamb, according to the house of his father, a lamb for a household. And if the household is too small for the lamb, let him and his neighbor next to his house take it according to the number of the persons; according to each man's need you shall make your count for the lamb. Your lamb shall be without blemish, a male of the first year. You may take it from the sheep or from the goats. Now you shall keep it until the fourteenth day of the same month. Then the whole assembly of the congregation of Israel shall kill it at twilight. And they shall take some of the blood and put it on the two doorposts and on the lintel of the houses where they eat it. Then they shall eat the flesh on that night; roasted in fire, with unleavened bread and with bitter herbs they shall eat it. Do not eat it raw, nor boiled at all with water, but roasted in fire—its head with its legs and its entrails. You shall let none of it remain until morning, and what *remains of it until morning you shall burn with fire. And thus you shall eat it: with a belt on your waist, your sandals on your feet, and your staff in your hand. So you shall eat it in haste. It is the Lord's Passover* (Ex. 12:1–11).

"So this day shall be to you a memorial; and you shall keep it as a feast to the Lord throughout your generations. You shall keep it as a feast by an everlasting ordinance. Seven days you shall eat unleavened bread. On the first day you shall remove leaven from your houses. For whoever eats leavened bread from the first day until the seventh day, that person shall be cut off from Israel. On the first day there shall be a holy convocation, and on the seventh day there shall be a holy convocation for you. No manner of work shall be done on them, but that which everyone must eat— that only may be prepared by you. So you shall observe the Feast of Unleavened Bread, for on this same day I will have brought your armies out of the land of Egypt. Therefore you shall observe this day throughout your generations as an everlasting ordinance. In the first month, on the fourteenth day of the month at evening, you shall eat unleavened bread, until the twenty-first day of the month at evening. For seven days no leaven shall be found in your houses, since whoever eats what is leavened, that same person shall be cut off from the congregation of Israel, whether he is a stranger or a native of the land. You shall eat nothing leavened; in all your dwellings you shall eat unleavened bread" (Ex. 12:14–20).

"These are the feasts of the Lord, holy convocations which you shall proclaim at their appointed times. On the

fourteenth day of the first month [Nisan] *at twilight is the Lord's Passover. And on the fifteenth day of the same month is the Feast of Unleavened Bread to the Lord; seven days you must eat unleavened bread. On the first day* [of the feast] *you shall have a holy convocation* [high sabbath]; *you shall do no customary work on it"* (Lev. 23:4–7).

There are two terms that get many people confused: Passover and the Feast of Unleavened Bread. Also, on the Jewish calendar the date changes at sundown. The Passover is a single day and begins at sundown at the end of the day of the thirteenth and continues until sundown on the day of the fourteenth. Sundown on the fourteenth marks the beginning of the Feast of Unleavened Bread which goes from the fifteenth of Nisan through the twenty-first of Nisan.

Jews were required to celebrate the Passover every year to remember the Exodus from Egypt. From the time of Moses, Jews have celebrated the Passover and the Feast of the Unleavened Bread in much the same way. The Passover meal is called a 'seder' and it means 'order' in Hebrew. There is a set order of the meal, and the steps have been used to explain the lessons from the Exodus.

The selection and preparation of the lamb is remarkably consistent between the Passover lamb, and Jesus, our sacrificial lamb. On the tenth of Nisan, the lamb is taken to the temple and examined by the priests to ensure that the lamb is male and without blemish. If the family did not have a lamb, one could be purchased at the temple. The lamb would be taken home to live with the family until the fourteenth. On the tenth of Nisan Jesus presented himself at the temple and was found to be without blemish.

Just as the Israelites were saved by the blood of the Passover lamb, so too are the believers in Jesus saved by the sacrifice on the cross to participate in the second Exodus, from the slavery of sin to the freedom as a child of God. "For indeed Christ, our Passover, was sacrificed for us" (1 Cor. 5:7).

On the thirteenth of Nisan the head of the household led the family in searching for leaven and removing it. In very orthodox families, the leaven bread was burned or destroyed. In less orthodox families, they would sell their bread to a gentile and buy it back after the week of the Feast of Unleavened bread.

After the house was cleaned of all leaven, the dining area was prepared with low (about eighteen-inch-tall), round tables and sufficient cushions for every guest to lay on the floor on their left side and reach their food with the right hand.

During the day of the thirteenth, each family would bring a lamb (that had been inspected on the tenth) to the temple to be sacrificed. At 3:00 p.m., a priest would blow the shofar (ram's horn) to announce the beginning of slaying of the lambs. In the case where the thirteenth is the day before the sabbath, the sacrifice would be done at 2:00 p.m. Some of the blood would be captured and the kidneys removed. These items were then taken to the altar as a burned sacrifice. Josephus claims that there were over 250,000 lambs sacrificed one year.[1] The lamb was prepared for roasting by skinning and not breaking any bones. It was then roasted by passing a stick through the length of the animal, and another across its front shoulders, forming a cross. All meal preparation had to be complete before sundown on the fourteenth when the high sabbath began.

At sundown on the fourteenth, the date became the fifteenth and Feast of the Unleavened Bread commenced and the family ate the Passover meal. This feast was a high holy sabbath and no work could be done. The criminals that were being crucified must be deceased and taken down off their crosses before the sabbath begins.

Passover Sequence:

A blessing is said over the first of four cups of wine. The first cup of wine is called the Cup of Sanctification and it is to commemorate the promise: "I will bring you out" (Exodus 6:6).

Everyone washes their hands before eating some appetizer. Each participant dips a vegetable into either salt water, vinegar, or charoset (sauce).

There are three loafs of unleavened bread called 'matzah'. The middle of the three is broken into two pieces. One of the broken halves is wrapped in a white cloth and hidden until after the meal. We often speak of the Father, Son, and Holy Ghost. Keep in mind that after Jesus was crucified (broken), he was wrapped in a while cloth and buried until his resurrection.

The host tells the Passover story; that is Israel's journey from slavery to freedom.

A second cup of wine is consumed. The second cup is called the Cup of Plagues and reflects the plagues that came upon Egypt. This relates to the second promise, "I will free you from being slaves" (Ex. 6:6).

Everyone washes their hands.

Bitter herbs are eaten. In Exodus 12:8 the Jews were told to eat the lamb with unleavened bread and with bitter herbs. In Hebrew, the bitter herbs are called 'maror' and they were usually grated horseradish.

The main course is roasted lamb.

A blessing is said after the meal.

The broken half of matzah, which had been hidden, is to be found by a child and brought back to the table. The matzah is broken into pieces and distributed. Everyone eats of the bread.

A third cup of wine is consumed. The third cup is called the Cup of Redemption as God says, "I will redeem you" (Exodus 6:6).

A child opens the door to see if Elijah is there. In Malachi 4:5–6 The Bible says that Elijah would come and precede the Messiah.

The 'Hallel', the praise psalms (Psalms 113 to 118) are sung.

A fourth cup of wine is consumed. The fourth cup is called the Cup Of Completion as God says, "I will take you as my own people" (Ex. 6:7).

The relationship between the Passover and Christ was initially fulfilled when Christ, the Lamb of God, was sacrificed to deliver us from the prison of sin. The future fulfillment of the Passover will be completed when Christ takes his flock to the Marriage Supper of the Lamb (Rev. 19:9).

CHAPTER TEN

TUESDAY DAYTIME, TWELFTH OF NISAN

Peter and John can be seen preparing for the Passover meal in Matthew 26:17–19, Mark 14:12–16, and Luke 22:7–13. The disciples asked, where will we eat the Passover dinner? Jesus told Peter and John to enter the city and they would meet a man carrying a water pitcher. They were to follow him and when he enters a house, tell the master of the house that the teacher wishes to use his upper room for the dinner. There is speculation that this was all pre-arranged and that the master of the house was a secret disciple like Nicodemus or Joseph of Arimathea. Many wealthy Jews were supporters of Jesus, but remained silent for fear of the Pharisees.

Peter and John went from Bethany to Jerusalem, met the man with the water pitcher, and followed him to his master's home. The master made available to them the upper room which was furnished with the cooking equipment and cushions for them to lie on while they ate. In short, the room was ready for their use.

The classic view is that they bought a lamb, took it to the temple to be slain in the court, cut it up, took the fat out to be burnt on the alter, and sprinkled its blood on the alter, and then took it back to the upper room to be roasted. They acquired the unleavened bread, wine, bitter herbs, and sauce called 'Charoseth', into which the herbs were dipped. The Passover meal was ready for Jesus and the disciples.

The problem is that John and Peter did their tasks Tuesday during the day and their meal occurred Tuesday night, the thirteenth of Nisan. The classic Passover meal was eaten on the evening on the fourteenth of Nisan.

In Luke 22:15, Jesus said, "With *fervent* desire I have desired to eat this Passover with you before I suffer [. . .]" This suggests that it was a classic Passover meal, just that there is no mention of the lamb, bitter herbs, or other components of the traditional Passover meal. It has been discussed in many commentaries that this was not a classic meal, but rather a dinner where Jesus established a new Passover custom of the bread and wine. Whichever is correct, it seems that Jesus did not follow the traditional seder or order of the meal.

CHAPTER ELEVEN

THE LAST SUPPER

Tuesday Night to Dawn Wednesday, the Thirteenth of Nisan

Leonardo da Vinci's picture of the Last Supper shows everyone sitting at a table, as Europeans would. Jewish tradition says that they lie or recline on couches on their left side so that they can use their right hand to eat with.

Passover with the Disciples – Matt. 26:20, Mark 14:17, Luke 22:14

Jesus and the twelve disciples (including Judas) went to the Upper Room and ate the Passover meal. During the meal, if this was a traditional Seder, they discussed the meaning of the Passover, including the lamb, the bitter herbs, and the unleavened bread.

Jesus Washes the Disciples' Feet – John 13:1–20

The act of washing feet was always done by the lowest servant, and rarely done by a Jew. The custom of washing feet was not used by the Jews at their Passover, nor at their private entertainments, or common meals. It was done at the reception of strangers or travelers, who had just come off a journey, whereby they had contracted dirt and filth. There are examples of the wife washing her husband's feet in 1 Samuel 25:41.

Jesus took off his outer garments and put a towel around himself and proceeded to wash the disciples' feet. When he came to Peter, Peter objected and asked, "Lord, are You washing my feet" (John 13:6). Peter could not understand why the Lord would stoop to wash his feet. Peter seemed to feel that Jesus was doing too much for such a worthless creature as Peter. Jesus said that he (Peter) did not understand what he was doing, but would in a short time. The lesson for us is that sometimes we must wait for the Lord to show us why things happen. In the meantime, we must patiently submit to the divine will.

Peter said, "You shall never wash my feet!" Jesus answered him, "If I do not wash you, you have no part with Me" (John 13:8). Jesus used the physical act of washing with water to explain the spiritual act of being washed by the blood of Jesus. We are washed by the blood of Jesus in order that we may have a part with him; spiritual fellowship with him now, and we have with him the undefiled inheritance for eternity. Peter then ask Jesus to not only was his feet, but his hands, and his head which could have meant that Peter knew of the general pollution of his nature, and that he needed a thorough spiritual cleaning by Jesus. Jesus said, "He who is bathed needs only to wash his feet, but is completely clean; and you are clean, but not all of you" (John 13:10). Gill says that once we have been cleaned by the blood of Jesus, we are totally clean. We will sin and then we need to be cleaned again by grace and justification. [1] The phrase "and you are clean, but not all of you" (John 13:10) means that eleven of the twelve disciples were clean, Judas being the exception. It is worth noting that Jesus washed all of the disciples' feet, including Judas'. Jesus knew that Judas would betray him, yet Jesus washed his feet.

When Jesus had finished washing the disciples' feet, he put back on his outer garments and sat down with the disciples. Jesus asks, "Do you know what I have done to you" (John 13:12). The disciples would finally understand after the cross, but in that moment, they would understand this as an act of humility and that they (we) were to serve one another. Jesus' message is that the greatest display of love is to serve. You will see kings and the Pope washing the feet of twelve poor people on Maundy Thursday as a display of their humility. Jesus' message is that we are to serve others daily, as part of our lives. The gospel is a life to be lived and not just an ideal to be contemplated.

Prediction of Betrayal – Matt. 26:20–25, Mark 14:17–21, Luke 22:21–23, John 13:18–30

Jesus was very agitated and troubled when he said, "one of you will betray me" (John 13:21). This is to say that one of you will turn me over to the chief priest and elders in order that I might be put to death. The disciples stared at one another, at a loss to know which one of them he meant. They could not imagine who would do such a thing. They all asked, "Lord, is it I" (Matt. 26:22). We are all quite capable of the worst sin. If we think otherwise, we are deluded and have no idea how much we owe to the grace of God.

Peter motions to John, who was lying next to Jesus, to convince him to ask Jesus who will betray him. In classic Jewish tradition, there would be multiple tables and around the tables were mats. Those eating would lie on their left side and eat with their right hand. The description of John's position (leaning on Jesus' bosom) indicates that John was lying next to Jesus' right hand. John leaned back and asked, "Lord, who is it"

(John 13:25). Since John was next to Jesus, Jesus may not have responded loudly, maybe just enough for John to hear. Jesus responded, "It is he to whom I shall give a piece of bread when I have dipped *it*" (John 13:26). Jesus then dipped the bread in the juice and handed it to Judas. Since Jesus is able to give the bread to his betrayer it is likely that Judas was next to Jesus, reclining at the same table. John says that when Judas accepted the bread, Satan entered him and he became totally committed to the betrayal. Jesus knew Judas' plan and said, "What you do, do quickly" (John 13:27). Judas departed to meet with the Pharisees so that they could execute their plan to arrest and crucify Jesus.

When Jesus told Judas (John 13:27) to do what he needed to do, the disciples assumed that he was being sent off to purchase the necessities for the Passover meal. If they were eating the Passover meal, why would the disciples think that Judas was leaving to purchase the supplies for the meal? It is not likely that Judas could have made the arrangements for Jesus' betrayal immediately after the Passover meal because all the heads of households would have been in their homes with their families for the meal.

Jesus Gives the New Commandment – John 13:31–35

After Judas departs, Jesus said, "Now the Son of Man is glorified, and God is glorified in Him. If God is glorified in Him, God will also glorify the Him in Himself, and glorify Him immediately" (John 13:31–32). Let us disassemble these two sentences. "The Son of Man" always refers to Jesus. Glorification can refer to either the giving of praise, or the manifestation of that which is worthy of praise. So, Jesus is now worthy of praise and Jesus has praised God. Jesus' act of submitting to the cross will lead God to praise Jesus, and God will do so quickly. The glory of God is great, in the salvation of his elect by the death of Jesus, in his wisdom and power, in his truth and faithfulness, in his justice and holiness, as well as his love, grace, and mercy.

In a very tender manner, Jesus then opens the door to the future a little wider. He says, "Little children, I shall be with you a little while longer. You will seek Me; and as I said to the Jews, 'Where I am going, you cannot come,' so now I say to you" (John 13:33). "Little children" puts the relationship between the disciples and Jesus in the same relationship that Jesus has with his Father. Jesus continued, "A new commandment I give to you, that you love one another; as I have loved you, that you also love one another. By this all will know that you are My disciples, if you have love for one another" (John 13:34–35). The love that Jesus is speaking of is not simply a feeling. One cannot really command a feeling. It is willingly doing the best for the other person (1 John 3:11–18). Since God's will alone is truly what is good in any situation, love acts in obedience to God's will, under the guidance of the Spirit.

The Disciples Argue About Greatness – Luke 22:24–30

The disciples discussed again which one of them was the greatest (Matt. 18:1). They apparently were still looking for the Messiah to take David's role and throw the Romans out of Israel. Their reasoning was that once Jesus had established himself as the leader, he would need assistants, and the disciples would fill that role. This shows how deep-seated the love of power and ambition is in us and how blind the disciples were to Jesus' crucifixion the next day.

Jesus asks who is greater, the one who sits at the table and eats, or the one who serves the meal. Obviously the one who sits, but did not Jesus just wash their feet? Jesus explains that greatness is not our position and power in life. Rather, greatness is demonstrated when we are humble and serve others. Jesus promised them a kingdom, just not one of this world, where they would sit at Jesus' table to eat and drink. They will all have thrones where they will judge the twelve tribes of Israel.

Prediction of Denial – Matt. 26:31–35, Mark 14:27–31, Luke 22:31–34, John 13:36–38

Peter appeared to have a strong desire to be close to Jesus and to stay with him, but he lacked the spiritual ear to understand what Jesus was saying. He wanted to know the physical location where Jesus would be so that he could be with him. Jesus assured him that he will follow later, when Peter was crucified in Rome. But Peter continued to protest and said that he would lay down his life for Jesus. Jesus' responded, "Will you lay down your life for My sake? Most assuredly, I say to you, the rooster shall not crow till you have denied Me three times" (John 13:38). But, it may not have been a rooster; the following excerpt is from "What if it Wasn't a Rooster" by Lonnie Lane:

> *Going back to the original Hebrew, the word 'rooster' or 'cock' may be a mistranslation. It also means 'man'. The Talmud (rabbinic law, not scriptural) which is supported by Josephus, chickens were forbidden in Jerusalem. There was a priest in charge of locking the Temple doors at night and then unlocking the doors each morning just before dawn. At that time, he would unlock the Temple and cry*

out for the priests to wake up and prepare for the morning sacrifice. He would also cry out for the people to come and worship. The crowing of a rooster would have had no spiritual significance in itself to Peter if that's what he had heard. But if Peter was hearing the call to sacrifice, the call to service, and the call to worship those words were likely to have brought the stunning revelation to him that he had failed on all three counts. Where was the willing sacrifice that Peter had so boldly proclaimed? Where was his calling to serve the Lord as he was sure he always would? And where was his worship now that he suddenly felt so far from Yeshua [Jesus], and so far from God?[2]

After what was said to Peter, the disciples were shaken. Peter did not always have the right answers, but his fierce loyalty to Jesus was very clear. If he was going to deny Jesus, what hope was there for the rest of them (and us)?

Supplies for the Road – Luke 22:35–38

Christ referred to his mission trip that the disciples were sent on in Matthew 10:5. Jesus asked in their prior missionary travels if they had need of anything? They said that had everything they needed for that trip.

In Verse 36, Jesus then said, "But now [. . .]" times have changed. They would need supplies, such as a money bag, knapsack, and sword. They would be on their own for the rest of their lives and would need supplies. In the countries they would be traveling to, they would encounter dangers and they would need a sword to protect themselves. The two points being made are that it is correct for ministers and missionaries to provide for their needs before set off on their journeys and that self-defense is lawful. When you are surrounded by danger, it is proper to defend your life. The disciples said that they had two swords among them. Jesus said, "It is enough" (Luke 22:38). Gill suggested in that Jesus was speaking ironically, "Only two swords for the eleven of you". It seems that they had no idea what was coming.[3]

Jesus is the Way to the Father – John 14: 1–7

Jesus then said, "Let not your heart be troubled; you believe in God, believe also in Me" (John 14:1). We can only find real hope and confidence by focusing on God rather than on ourselves. Look up, not in! Jesus continued, "In my Father's house are many mansions" (John 14:2). The Greek word for mansions is "monay", which means "a staying, abiding, dwelling, abode", which is a mistranslation from our current understanding of castle or some physical, magnificent dwelling place. The disciples were locked into the physical world, and had a serious lack of understanding of the spiritual one. Thomas, whom we know as doubting Thomas, said, "Lord, we do not know where you are going, and how can we know the way" (John 14:5). Jesus said, "I am the way, the truth, and the life. No one comes to the Father except through me" (John 14:6) This is the central point, the core, the nucleus of the Gospel.

The Father Revealed – John 14:7–11

Jesus then talked of the future, "If you had known Me, you would have known My Father also" (John 14:7). But Philip said that if Jesus would show him the Father that would be sufficient for him. I guess so! Jesus seems to become a little frustrated with Philip, and asks, "Have I been with you so long [three years], and yet you have not known Me, Philip? He who has seen Me has seen the Father; so how can you say, 'Show us the Father'? Do you not believe that I am in the Father, and the Father in Me? The words that I speak to you I do not speak on My own *authority;* but the Father who dwells in Me does the works [miracles].Believe Me that I *am* in the Father and the Father in Me, or else believe Me for the sake of the works themselves" (John 14: 9–11). Jesus does not represent the Father, he presents him.

The Answered Prayer – John 14:12–14

We often pray in "Jesus' name", but his actual instruction is, "And whatever you ask in My name, that I will do, that the Father may be glorified in the Son" (John 14:13). The promise is made to those who will pray in Jesus' name and for the glory of the Father. Jesus continued, "If you ask anything in My name, I will do *it*" (John 14:14), so that the Father gets the glory. To believe that we will get whatever we ask is self-idolatry and is the very opposite of what Jesus is teaching. To God goes the glory. As such, it is great promise for the advancement of God's purposes in oneself, in the church, and in the world.

Jesus Promises Another Helper – John 14:15–18

Jesus said, "If you love Me, keep My commandments" (John 14:15). This is not to question his disciples love or devotion, but as a reminder to all that we are to do what he says, including following his way of life. Jesus continued, "And I will pray the Father, and He will give you another Helper" (John 14:16). Jesus was a comforter, and he is promised another Comforter, the Holy Spirit. This is a clear reference to the Trinity: the Father is prayed unto, The Son in human form is praying, and the Holy Spirit, the Comforter, is prayed for.

Jesus then promised that he would not leave them as orphans, but that he would come to them after his death through his resurrection.

Indwelling of the Father and the Son – John 14:19–21

"A little while longer and the world will see Me no more [with their earthly eyes], *but you will see Me* [after the resurrection for forty days and then as the Holy Spirit]. *Because I live, you will live also* [the disciples would be united with Jesus through the Holy Spirit because Jesus is the Holy Spirit]. *At that day you will know that I am in My Father, and you in Me, and I in you* [the Trinity is the Father, Jesus, and Holy Spirit wrapped together as one except they are three]. *He who has My commandments and keeps them, it is he who loves Me* [if you love Jesus, you will keep his way of life]. *And he who loves Me will be loved by My Father, and I will love him and manifest Myself to him* [through the Holy Spirit]*"* (John 14:19–21).

Obedience and Love – John 14:22–24

Judas (not Iscariot) asked Jesus, "Lord, how is it that You will manifest Yourself to us, and not to the world" (John 14:22). Jesus responded by explaining that one obeys what one loves. Indeed, our patterns of obedience reveal what we really love. Jesus was going way beyond obeying a law, He was saying that we are to incorporate his teaching into the core principles of our lives. If we do incorporate his teaching into our core beliefs, the Father will love us and the Trinity will make its home in us. The Greek word for home (monay) is the same Greek word from verse 2 when Jesus was describing "mansions". If we do not love Jesus, we will not incorporate this teaching into our lives. Jesus then stated that the words he had spoken were not his words, but the Father's. If we reject Jesus' words, we have rejected the Father.

The Gift of His Peace – John 14:25–28

Jesus continued by saying that while he was with them, he taught them about the Holy Spirit. He promised that the Father would send the Holy Spirit in his name, and the helper (Holy Spirit) would continue teaching and helping them remember what he had said. Jesus then promised the disciples that they would have his calmness and confidence that comes from union with God and faith in him and his purposes. Jesus was teaching that although they (we) would go through trials and troubles and many would suffer a martyr's death, they (we) would have God's peace and confidence. Jesus then repeats what he said in verse 1, "Let not you heart be troubled, neither let it be afraid" (John14:27). Fear is the opposite of faith. Fear destroys faith, and faith overcomes fear. Those who have faith in the final outcome have nothing to fear, as proven by the cross and then the resurrection. Jesus had faith in the final outcome, and did not fear the cross. Jesus restated that he was going away *and* that he was returning to them, first physically and then via the Holy Spirit. The knowledge that he was returning to the Father filled him with joy, and if the disciples truly loved him, they would be filled with joy too.

Jesus Talks about Satan Failing – John 14:29–31

Jesus told the disciples that he had told them these things before they happened, so that when the events unfolded, they would know and understand the final outcome. Jesus continued by saying that the end was near and that the ruler of the world (Satan) was coming for him, but Satan would not find any sin in him. Jesus took on himself the sins of the world, but no sin was in him. According to the very first prophecy in Genesis 3:15, Satan bruised Jesus' heel (did not significantly hurt him), Jesus bruised Satan's head (did significant harm to Satan that would eventually would destroy him). Jesus closes by stating that the world must know that he loves the Father, and does exactly what the Father tells him to do. Jesus then said, "Arise, let us go from here." (John 14:31)

CHAPTER TWELVE

JESUS AND THE DISCIPLES GO TO GETHSEMANE

Tuesday Night to Dawn Wednesday, the Thirteenth of Nisan

It appears that Jesus and the disciples left the upper room and were heading towards the Garden of Gethsemane. While they were walking to Gethsemane, Jesus continued teaching.

The True Vine – John 15:1–8

"I am the true vine, and My Father is the vinedresser. Every branch in Me that does not bear fruit He takes away, and every branch that bears fruit He prunes, that it may bear more fruit" (John 15:1–2).

The vine was always a symbol of Israel. Josephus, *Antiquities of the Jews,* describes a golden grapevine over the door to the temple.[1] Jeremiah 2:21 complains that Israel has turned into a wild vine, turned to bitterness. Isaiah 5:4 talks about a vineyard that produces wild grapes (bitter), and that it shall be burned.

When Jesus says that "I am the true vine" (John 15:1), he is saying that the people of God is no longer exclusively the nation of Israel, but the followers of Jesus, world-wide (including Israel). If a branch (Israel) does not produce fruit, it will be cut off and burned. The image of fruit symbolizes that which is at the heart of both Christian witness and ethics, union with God.

In verse John 15:3, Jesus said, "You are already clean because of the word which I have spoken to you." This does not mean that the disciples were perfect, but that they had been under a process of purifying by his instructions all the time that Jesus had been with them. Also, Judas had been removed from their group (John 13:10).

Jesus continued his vine metaphor by saying that we, the branches, can do nothing unless we are drawing our energy and strength from him. Jesus said, "If you abide in Me, and My words abide in you" (John15:7). This does not only mean that you have a basic knowledge of his words. It means that his words must be a living principle and regulate your affections and life. If this is true, then "[. . .] you will ask what you desire, and it shall be done for you. By this My Father is glorified [honored]" (John 15:7–8).

Love and Joy Perfected – John 15:9–17

We do not have the ability to totally comprehend the Father's love for his Son, but this is how Jesus loved his disciples and us. He directed all of us to live in this love and follow his commandments, just as he lives in the Father's love and he follows the Father's commandments and is totally submissive to the Father's will.

Jesus commands that we love one another as much as he loves us. There is no greater demonstration of one's love for another than to lay down their life for them. Jesus loves us so much that he went to the cross so that we might live.

Jesus told the disciples that they are no longer his servants, rather, they are his friends. As such, he has shared all things that the Father has shown him (his coming death, resurrection, and ascension). The disciples did not seek out Jesus, instead he sought them out and appointed them as his disciples. Their role would be to evangelize the world and create a new worldwide religion. We all have been given (chosen) special skills and talents and it is our responsibility to use those skills and bear fruit. Jesus then repeated the promise that whatever we ask the Father for in his name, the Father will give to us. Jesus also repeated his command that we are to love one another.

The World's Hatred – John 15:18–25

We should not, we must not expect the earth dwellers' (the unsaved whose home is on this earth) love. The Son of God was hated, we should not expect better. The earth dwellers' love their own kind, but will never love those who follow the Son of man. The earth dwellers live in a dark place, but we bring light to their world and expose their filth. Because we have exposed their world, they will hate us, Jesus, and the Father. Jesus reminds the disciples (and us) that the nature of earth dwellers' is to hate that which is different from them. Jesus is referencing Psalms 69:4.

Jesus Speaks on the Holy Spirit – John 15:26–27

Jesus reminds the disciples that the Holy Spirit will come and remind them about Jesus' time with them and that they will give an eyewitness testimony through their preaching and writing.

Warning of Jewish and Christian Persecution – John 16:1–4

Jesus has warned the disciples and us so that we won't be surprised when persecuted and caused to stumble. He warned that they would be excommunicated from the synagogues and that when the religious leaders kill Jesus, disciples, Stephen, and us, they believe that they are doing a service for God. The religious leaders (Saul) will do these things because they do not really understand the Father or Jesus. Please note that John 16:3 is the opposite of John 3:16. Jesus said that they [the disciples] had been warned, so that when their [persecution] time comes they would remember the warning. He explained that in the beginning he did not warn them [the disciples] because he was with them to protect them, but soon they will be on their own, depending on the Holy Spirit.

The Work of the Holy Spirit – John 16:5–15

Jesus stated that he was going away, but no one asked, "Where are you going?" One common thread through the commentaries is that the disciples were consumed in their grief and not considering where he was going. He explained that it was to their advantage that he depart, because the Holy Spirit cannot (would not) come to them unless/until Jesus completed the mission.

It is often necessary that God needs to put us through severe affliction before our pride will be humbled and we are willing and able to understand the plainest truths. Remember John 15:2, that the vine dresser prunes the vine to produce more fruit. We do not enjoy being pruned or suffering affliction, but God is cutting away those parts that distract us from him. Only after we have been properly humbled and tenderized can he use us. This is what the disciples were struggling with. They visualized a Davidic kingdom, which included removing the Romans and reestablishing their autonomy. Jesus' kingdom is not physical and he had to suffer through death, resurrection, and ascension before the Holy Spirit would be able to open the disciples' minds so that they could comprehend the truth.

Sorrow Will Turn to Joy – John 16:16–24

"A little while [Mikron, a Greek word referring to a very small amount of time, in this case it means the next day], and you will not see Me; and again a little while [three days after that], and you will see me, because I go to the Father" (John 16:16). From our perspective, after the fact, we have no difficulty in understanding this statement, but the disciples were totally confused and were asking each other what Jesus meant. Jesus asked, "Are you inquiring among yourselves about what I said" (John 16:19). He continued by telling them that they will weep ('klaio', a Greek word meaning morning for the dead), and the Jews will be happy, but that the disciple's grief will turn to joy when they see him again. Jesus is clearly telling them that He will die, be resurrected, and they will be filled with joy.

Jesus has Overcome the World – John 16:25–33

Jesus said that he had been talking in figurative speech, and that it was time for straight talking. He let his followers know: I came from the Father, entered the world, I am now leaving the world, and I am now going back to the Father.

The disciples thanked Jesus for his straight talking and stated that they now (finally) believe that He came from God. Jesus challenged this statement by asking, "Do you now believe" (John 16:31). Do you really, truly believe? They did not know what was coming and that every one of them would scatter to stay out of harm's way. Every one of us must ask ourselves, when confronted with the option, will we deny Christ and scatter, or will we stand fast and accept the martyr's fate with Jesus' name on our lips? This is happening today as our brothers and sisters in the middle east are having their throats cut.

Jesus' High Priestly Prayer – John 17

John 17 is devoted to Jesus' prayer for himself, the disciples and for all believers. Jesus and the disciples are finishing their walk from the upper room to the Garden of Gethsemane. It is the longest prayer recorded in the New Testament.

Jesus Prays for Himself – John 17:1–5

Jesus lifts his eyes to heaven and says, "Father, the hour has come" (John 17:1) for his suffering and death. He asks the Father to honor him so that he could honor the Father. In other words, the Father's glorification of the Son is giving the Son authority over all flesh. The Son will glorify the Father through giving eternal life to those the Father gives him. Jesus said that he had honored the Father while he was on earth, and that he had finished his mission. Jesus asks to be glorified with the Father, with the glory which he had before the creation.

Jesus Prays for His Disciples – John 17:6–19

Jesus says that he revealed the Father to the disciples and they believed what Jesus revealed, including that Jesus is the Son of God sent by the Father. Jesus continued by saying that his mission was complete and no longer part of this wicked world, but the disciples would remain and would need the Father's protection. Those that the Father gave Jesus are all still with Jesus, except for Judas (the son of perdition). Jesus kept them all safe, and he asked the Father to protect them from the evil one. Jesus asked that they might be made more holy and set apart as ministers and teachers of God's kingdom. Ministers of the gospel would be really devoted to the service of God in proportion as they are personally pure.

Jesus Prays for all Believers – John 17:20–26

Jesus expands his prayer to include all those who will believe the disciples' teaching. We value the prayers of our friends, and especially the prayers of our minister. How much should we value this prayer? Jesus is praying for each of us, the Son of God prayed for each of us! All of us who are children of God are brothers and sisters. We should act like heavenly brothers and sisters, not as earthly ones. There may be denominational differences, but we are all the bride of Christ.

CHAPTER THIRTEEN

GARDEN OF GETHSEMANE

Tuesday Night to Dawn Wednesday, the Thirteenth of Nisan

Immediately after Jesus' prayer (discussed in the previous chapter), he and the disciples enter the Kidron Valley which is the entrance to garden of Gethsemane and the Mount of Olives. This means that they have transited from the Upper Room where the Last Supper was held, through the city, and out a gate.

Prayer in the Garden – Matt. 26:36–46, Mark 14:32–42, Luke 22:39–46, John 18:1–2

The Garden of Gethsemane is also an olive grove and the name suggests an olive press. This was a place that Jesus often retired to and it was well known that he liked to retire here. He directed the disciples to rest and pray that they would not enter into temptation. Jesus took Peter, James, and John further into the grove. These three had seen sights that the others had not seen: the raising of Jairus' daughter and the transfiguration. It is important to remember that it took three witnesses for an event to be established.

Jesus told these three disciples to remain alert and to guard him against danger. He then continued a short distance and fell down on his face in prayer. Luke says that an angel came to strengthen him. Jesus prayed in agony, "O My Father [Abba, daddy], if it is possible, let this cup pass from Me; nevertheless, not as I will, but as You will" (Matt. 26:39). Luke says that the sweat fell from Jesus like drops of blood. He did not say that Jesus sweat blood, just that sweat dropped off him like blood. Jesus was not eager to proceed with his mission, but he accepted the Father's will. Jesus returned to the three and found them asleep. He woke up Peter and said, "What! Could you not watch with Me one hour" (Matt. 26:40). Jesus was obviously frustrated and told Peter to watch and pray lest he enter into temptation. Peter needed strength to stand up for Jesus and not deny him, but Peter only wanted to sleep.

Jesus departed them and went back to pray. He again asked if the cup could be passed from him, but that the Father's will be done. Jesus returned to the three and found them asleep again. This time he returned to his place and continued praying. He returned again and found them all sleeping. Again, in frustration, Jesus asked, "Are *you* still sleeping and resting" (Matt. 26:45). The hour of Jesus' betrayal was at hand.

Betrayal in Gethsemane – Matt. 26:47–56, Mark 14:43–50, Luke 22:47–53, John 18:3–12

While Jesus was waking up the disciples, Judas accompanied by the temple guards, Roman soldiers who were assigned to the temple, and others came into the garden. The guards had their weapons, but the others seemed to have picked up whatever they could lay their hands on. It was the day before Passover, the moon was nearly full and it should have been bright, but they brought lanterns and torches. There may have been clouds, and the garden had olive trees which may have made moonlight visibility poor.

John says that when the crowd approached, Jesus asked, "Whom are you seeking" (John 18:4). Jesus knew who they were seeking, he just wanted them to identify their primary target so that there would be an escape for the disciples. They responded, "Jesus of Nazareth" (John 18:5). Jesus said, "I am He" (John 18:5). The crowd seemed to be surprised and fell back either in shock or awe. Jesus again asked, "Whom are you seeking" (John 18:7). Again, they responded, "Jesus of Nazareth" (John 18:7). Jesus repeated, "I have told you that I am He. Therefore, if you seek Me, let these go their way" (John 18:8). He was referring to the disciples and he wanted them to be safe. Mark 14:51 talks about a young man who didn't slip away and was almost arrested. The guards wanted to arrest the entire group, but Jesus protected them.

Judas' prearranged signal was that he would kiss the one to be arrested. Judas greeted Jesus by calling him "rabbi", and kissed him on the cheek. Jesus asked, "Friend, why have you come" (Matt. 26:50). and the guards took Jesus into custody. John tells us that it was Peter who drew his sword and cut off the ear from Malchus, a servant of the high priest. Jesus immediately re-attached and healed his ear. Jesus said to Peter, "Put your sword into the sheath. Shall I not drink the cup which my father has given me?" (John 18:11)

It has been suggested that Matthew, Mark, and Luke wrote this while Peter was living to conceal his identity. By the time that John wrote this, Peter had been crucified. Jesus told Peter to put his sword away before the guards drew theirs and a fight ensued. This could have become a bloody brawl with Jesus and the disciples killed by the temple and Roman guards. It was not

God's plan for Jesus and the disciples to die by the sword. Jesus said that he could ask his Father for help and there would be twelve legions (72,000) of angels to protect him. But this was not God's plan. Jesus asked the guards, "Have you come out, as against a robber, with swords and clubs to take Me? I was daily with you in the temple teaching, and you did not seize Me. But the Scriptures must be fulfilled" (Mark 14:48–49).

Naked Young Man Escapes – Mark 14:51–52

This gives a glimpse into what would have happened if the disciples had not made their escape when Jesus said, "Therefore, if you seek Me, let these go their way" (John 18:8). Jesus provided an escape for the disciples, but this young man didn't run away. The young men (Roman guards) tried to grab him, but only succeeded in grabbing his linen sleeping garment and the young man escaped naked. There are those who believe that this young man was in fact Mark.

CHAPTER FOURTEEN

JEWISH JUDICIAL PROCEDURE VIOLATED

Tuesday Night to Dawn Wednesday, the Thirteenth of Nisan

An important lesson is that when a group of people have power and dogmatic certainty that their cause is right, they will prove to be a deadly enemy against those who do not play by their rules. These people believe that the end justifies the means. The following list of violations were extracted from an article titled: "The Trial of Jesus" by Dr. Graves.[1]

There were *many* violations of Jewish trial laws.

The Sanhedrin was charged under rabbinical law with the duty to protect and defend the accused. The law required the court to give accused persons "the benefit of doubt" and to assist the accused to establish his innocence.

Self-incrimination was prohibited. No one could be forced to admit guilt.

The defendant is considered presumed innocent until found guilt. The binding of any person before he was condemned was unlawful unless resistance was offered or expected. Jesus offered none.

It was illegal for judges to participate in the arrest of the accused. In Jesus' case, they arranged it.

Trials could not be conducted at night, the eve of a sabbath, or festival day.

When the witnesses' testimony was inconsistent, Jesus should have been released.

The High Priest puts Jesus under oath (Matthew 26:63) and asks if he is the Son of God. The high priest must be wearing his priestly robes to put anyone under oath. When Jesus affirms that he is the Son of God, the high priest declares this as blasphemy and tears his robes. It was unlawful for the high priest to tear his priestly robes (Leviticus 21:10).

The high priest declares that Jesus has spoken blasphemy and asks those present what he deserves. They say "death". A verdict must be done by roll call, with the youngest voting first.

There are more, but this list demonstrates the point that legal procedure does not matter when the end justifies the means.

CHAPTER FIFTEEN

FIRST TRIAL OF JESUS – ANNAS: TUESDAY NIGHT TO DAWN WEDNESDAY, THE THIRTEENTH OF NISAN

Annas Trials – John 18:12–24

Jesus was first taken to Annas, probably the most respected and powerful of the Jewish authorities at that time. Annas served as high priest from 6 to 15 AD when he was disposed by the Roman Governor, Valerius Gratus. Annas was the vice president of the Sanhedrin and was the patriarch of a family that held the office of high priest as late as 62 AD. Five of his sons and son-in-laws' were high priests. Caiaphas was his son-in-law and he had been installed by the Romans that same year. Remember, Caiaphas said it was expedient that one man should die for the people (John 11:49–50). Jesus did truly die for the people, just not quite how Caiaphas meant.

Peter and John followed Jesus to Annas' house. It seems that John was known either by Annas or his staff. It may be that John, being a fisherman, sold fish to them and was thus known. Anyway, because John was known by Annas' household staff, he was allowed to enter into the courtyard, but Peter was left outside. John came back to the door and talked to the girl who controlled the entrance into the courtyard. John got her to permit Peter to enter, but as he was passing through the doorway, she seemed to recognize him and ask, "You are not also *one* of this Man's disciples, are you" (John 18:17). By saying "also", she indicates that she knew that John was a disciple, and was asking Peter "are you one too?". It does not seem that Peter was under any threat, just that she was inquiring. Just a few hours earlier Peter said he would die for Jesus (John 13:37), now he does not want to be associated with him. Peter responded to the girl, "I am not" (John 18:17). Peter entered the courtyard and stood by a fire to keep warm.

This is not a real trial; there are no witnesses, no jury, and no sentence. This is more like a police interrogation of a newly arrested criminal before any formal procedures are begun. Annas interrogates Jesus about his disciples and doctrine. Jesus responded, "I spoke openly to the world. I always taught in synagogues and in the temple, where the Jews always meet, and in secret I have said nothing. Why do you ask Me? Ask those who have heard Me what I said to them. Indeed they know what I said" (John 18:20–21). One of the officers slapped him and said that was no way to talk to the high priest (Annas). Jesus said, "If I have spoken evil, bear witness of the evil; but if well, why do you strike Me" (John 18:23). In other words, "If I have lied, produce the witnesses. If you don't have witnesses, then I must be telling the truth and why are you striking me?". This is Jesus' demand for a fair trial, since in Jewish law the witnesses are questioned, not the accused.

Annas apparently heard enough and sent Jesus to Caiaphas. Jesus was still tied up (bound) at this point.

CHAPTER SIXTEEN

SECOND TRIAL – CAIAPHAS: TUESDAY NIGHT TO DAWN WEDNESDAY, THE THIRTEENTH OF NISAN

Jesus and Caiaphas – Matt. 26:57–68, Mark 14:53–72, Luke 22:54–65

Jesus was forcibly taken to Caiaphas, the current high priest where some of the Sanhedrin was assembled. Information on Caiaphas can be found throughout the Bible and other historical texts. We know that when Peter and John were arrested, Caiaphas was still the high priest (Acts 4:6).

Between midnight and dawn, Caiaphas and some of the members of Sanhedrin tried to find someone who would testify against Jesus so that they would have a legal reason to put him to death. Their intent was not to have a fair trial; they wanted an excuse to put Jesus to death. They brought many forward to testify, but none could produce testimony that would justify their desire to kill Jesus. They finally found two that could testify that Jesus said that he could destroy the temple and rebuild it in three days. He was referring, of course, to his crucifixion and resurrection in three days, but they did not understand that. Throughout all this, Jesus stood silent.

Jesus Proclaims that He is the Son of God – Matt. 26:63

Finally Caiaphas put Jesus under oath and commanded Jesus to answer him, "I put you under oath by the living God: Tell us if You are the Christ, the Son of God" (Matt. 26:63). Under Jewish law, if the high priest said, "I put you under oath by the living God," the accused *had to* answer (Lev. 5:1). The high priest cut to the root of the question, "Are you the Son of God?" Jesus responded, "It is as you said [yes]. Nevertheless, I say to, hereafter you will see the Son of Man [himself] sitting at the right hand of the Power [God], and coming on the clouds of heaven" (Matt. 26:64). Jesus said that he was the Son of God, and in the Jewish mind that was blasphemy of the highest degree.

When Jesus affirmed that He was the Son of God, the high priest declared it as blasphemy, tore his robes, and asked those present what Jesus deserved. It was unlawful for the high priest to tear his priestly robes (Lev. 21:10). The people said, "[. . .] death" (Matt. 26:66). However, a verdict had to be done by roll call, with the youngest voting first. Jesus was then blindfolded, they spat on him, slapped him, and demanded that he identify who struck him.

Peter's Denials

Peter had followed the guards from Annas' to Caiaphas' house and sat with the servants where a fire had been lit. John wrote that Peter's first denial was at Annas' house, but Matthew, Mark, and Luke do not discuss Annas' house and have Peter denying three times in Caiaphas' courtyard. According to Matthew, Mark, and Luke, Peter was sitting outside in the courtyard when a servant girl came to him and said that Peter was with Jesus. Mark has a rooster crow here. Peter denied Jesus. Then another girl said that Peter was with Jesus. This time Peter denied Jesus with an oath. Sometime later (Luke says one hour), some people came to Peter and said that his speech betrayed him as being one of them. John says that it was a relative of the man whose ear was cut off by Peter. This time Peter cursed and swore saying, "I do not know the Man" (Matt. 26:74). Immediately a rooster crowed.

Whether it is a fowl or a priest opening up the temple for morning worship, we are not certain. Luke said that Jesus turned and looked at Peter. In that moment, Peter realized what he had done and went outside the courtyard and wept bitterly. Failure, though painful, can be a means of growth; by God's grace we can learn from our mistakes.

CHAPTER SEVENTEEN

THIRD TRIAL – CAIAPHAS AND THE FULL SANHEDRIN: WEDNESDAY DAYTIME, THE THIRTEENTH OF NISAN

Jesus is Questioned Again – Matt 27:1, Mark 15:1, Luke 22:66–71

When morning had come, Jesus was taken to the temple, to the place where the Sanhedrin sat, known as "the paved stone chamber".[1] The Sanhedrin plotted to find legal grounds to kill Jesus. They said, "If you are the Christ, tell us" (Luke 22:67). Jesus responded by saying, "If I tell you, you will by no means believe. And if I also ask *you*, you will by no means answer Me or let *Me* go. Hereafter [after all this] the Son of Man [Jesus] will sit on the right hand of the power of God" (Luke 22:67). Then they asked if Jesus was the Son of God and Jesus responded that he was. The Sanhedrin had their excuse of blasphemy and the penalty for this was death. However, they did not have the authority to execute someone and they had to make their case to the Roman governor, Pontius Pilate.

In 7 AD, Herod Archelaus was replaced by a Roman procurator named Cponius. The legal power of the Sanhedrin was immediately restricted and the adjudication of capital cases was lost.[2] When the Sanhedrin found themselves deprived of their right over life and death, they covered their heads with ashes, their bodies with sackcloth, and bemoaned, "Woe unto us for the scepter has departed from Judah and the Messiah has not come".[3] The term "Scepter" refers to their tribal identity and the Sanhedrin's right to enforce Mosaic Laws and adjudicate capital offenses. The Sanhedrin thought that the word of God was broken. Genesis 49:10 says that: "The scepter shall not depart from Judah, [. . .] until the Shiloh [Messiah] comes". What they did not realize was that the Messiah was living in Nazareth.

Judas Hangs Himself – Matt. 27:3–5

Judas' remorse at Jesus' conviction by the Sanhedrin seems to indicate that he was surprised at the events. Likely, Judas expected Jesus to extract himself through a miracle and take on the role of a conquering messiah (David like figure). Instead, Judas was engulfed by the horrors of a guilty conscious and tried to undo his sin without seeking forgiveness from Jesus. Judas took the thirty pieces of silver, went to the temple and said, "I have sinned by betraying innocent blood" (Matt. 27:4). He knew that Jesus had not done anything wrong. Judas had been with him for nearly three years; he had heard Jesus' public preaching and his private teaching. Jesus was sinless, and Judas knew this. The hypocrisy of the priests is evident when they said, "What is that to us? You see to it" (Matt. 27:4). They were willing to pay blood money for Jesus' capture, but they were too religious to accept their own money back into their treasury. We can see this is Matthew 27:6–8:

> *But the chief priests took the silver pieces, and said, "It is not lawful for to put them into the treasury, because they are the price of blood." And they consulted together and bought with them the potter's field, to bury strangers in. Therefore that field has been called the Field of Blood to this day.*

Remember that Zechariah 11:12–13 was a prophecy of this very event. The prophecy specified the price as thirty pieces of silver (the established cost of a slave), the location as the temple also called the "House of the Lord", and who ends up with the money (the potter).

Prophecy Fulfilled – Matt. 27:9–10

"Then was fulfilled that which was spoken by Jeremiah the prophet" (Matt. 27:9). This is a series of scrolls, of which Zechariah is one. Matthew 27:9–10 continued, "And they took the thirty pieces of silver, the value of Him that was priced, whom they of the children of Israel priced, and gave them for the potter's field, as the Lord directed me."

I can imagine the desperate scream from Judas, crying helplessly at his sin, knowing that he had betrayed the Son of God. In terrible agony and remorse, Judas went out of the temple and hanged himself.

> *(Now this man purchased a field with the wages of iniquity; and falling headlong, he burst open in the middle and all his entrails gushed out. And it became known to all those dwelling in Jerusalem, so that field is called in their own language, Akel Dama, that is, Field of Blood)* (Acts 1:18–19).

CHAPTER EIGHTEEN

FOURTH TRIAL – PONTIUS PILATE FIRST: WEDNESDAY DAYTIME, THE THIRTEENTH OF NISAN

Pontius Pilate served as the sixth Roman procurator of Judaea from 26 to 36 AD, after which he was recalled to Rome and disappeared from history. He was hated by the Jews and he never really understood them. He ruled Judea in a reckless and arbitrary fashion. In 36 AD, he was deposed by Bitellius and sent to Rome where he was tried by Caligula. The tradition is that he killed himself, but the Coptic church came to believe that he became a Christian. By some of the things he did and said during and after his second trial of Jesus, I can see the Coptic viewpoint.[1]

The Trail – Matt. 27: 2, Mark 15:1, Luke 23:1–7

Matthew has a single verse that may relate to this first trial. Mark and John seem to skip this trial entirely. Luke is the only one that discusses it briefly.

The Sanhedrin takes Jesus to Pilate and accuse him of many crimes, hoping that one of their charges would get Pilate to crucify Jesus. Some of the crimes they accused him of are perverting the nation, forbidding the citizens from paying taxes to Caesar, and Christ claiming that he was a King. Frustrated, the Sanhedrin finally said that Jesus stirred up the people throughout all of Judea, from Galilee all the way down to Jerusalem. When Pilate heard that Jesus was from Galilee, he saw an opportunity to pass him off to Herod, who happened to be in Jerusalem for the Passover. Pilate directed that Jesus be taken to Herod for trial.

CHAPTER NINETEEN

FIFTH TRIAL – HEROD ANTIPAS: WEDNESDAY DAYTIME, THE THIRTEENTH OF NISAN

Herod's Trial – Luke 23:8–12

Luke is the only disciple that discusses Herod's trial. Herod is hoping for a show and to witness some miracle for himself. However Jesus is not an entertainer and stands silent as Herod questions him. Caiaphas angrily accused Jesus of many crimes, but Jesus remained silent. Herod and his guard treated Jesus with contempt, adorned him with a royal robe, and everyone was sent back to Pilate. Luke says that previous to this event, Pilate and Herod did not get along very well. But after this they were friends.

CHAPTER TWENTY

SIXTH TRIAL – PONTIUS PILATE SECOND: WEDNESDAY DAYTIME, THE THIRTEENTH OF NISAN

The Trial – Matt. 27:2 & 11–14, Mark 15:2–5, Luke 23:13–17, John 18:28–38

John provides the most complete description of this trial, and so I have elected to draw the material from him. The priests and elders would not enter the Hall of Judgment (Praetorium) because doing so would pollute them and they would have to re-perform ritual cleaning before they could partake in the Passover. Pilate went out of the Hall of Judgment, meet with the Jews and asked, "What accusation do you bring against this Man?" They responded, "If He were not an evildoer, we would not have delivered Him up to you" (John 18:29–30). It seems that in past cases, the Sanhedrin would try the case and present the convict to Pilate for his approval and execution. This time, Pilate took a personal interest and heard the evidence for himself. Likely, Pilate had heard of Jesus and he seemed to have a positive opinion of him. He knew that the

Sanhedrin had presented Jesus out of envy and Pilate was not disposed to *rubber stamp* their decision. Pilate said, "You take Him and Judge Him according to your law" (John 18:31). But the Jews said that they did not have the authority to execute convicted persons.

Pilate re-entered the Hall of Judgment and called for Jesus to be brought before him. Pontius Pilate asked Jesus, "Are You the King of the Jews" (John 18:33). Jesus responded, "Are you speaking for yourself about this, or did others tell you this concerning Me" (John 18:34). Pilate had no evidence that Jesus was a threat to Rome, he only had a demand from the Sanhedrin for the execution. It seemed that Pilate was getting frustrated with the events and Jesus' response. Pilate said, "Am I a Jew? Your own nation and the chief priests have delivered You to me. What have You done" (John 18:35). Jesus did not give a direct answer, but said, "My kingdom is not of this world. If my Kingdom were of this world, My servants would fight, so that I should not be delivered to the Jews; but now My kingdom is not from here" (John 18:36). Pilate repeats his question, "Are You a king then" (John 18:37). Jesus answered, "You say *rightly* that I am a king. For this cause I was born, and for this cause I have come into the world, that I should bear witness to the truth. Everyone who is of the truth hears My voice" (John 18:37). Imagine how frustrated Pilate was; he said, "What is truth" (John 18:38) and walked back to the Jewish crowd and spoke, "I find no fault in Him at all" (John 18:38).

Taking Barabbas' Place – Matt. 27:15–26, Mark 15:6–15, Luke 23:13–25, John 18:39–40

It was a custom of Rome to permit one person to be set free during the Passover time to soften the yoke that they lived under. Bar-Abbas (the son of Abbas) was a leader of an insurrection and had committed murder. Pilate offered to set Barabbas or Jesus free and gave it to the crowd for them to select. The crowd yelled for Barabbas to be set free. Pilate asked what should be done with Jesus, and they responded, "crucify him" (Mark 15:13). Pilate asked why the crowd wanted this, but the crowd continued to call for him to be crucified. Luke says that Pilate asked three times about releasing Jesus, but the crowd kept calling for Barabbas to be released. It is recorded that Pilate's wife warned him and said that he should, "Have nothing to do with that just Man, for I have suffered many things today in a dream because of Him" (Matt. 27:19).

Jesus took Barabbas' place on the cross, just as He took yours and mine. We all deserve the cross, but Jesus took our place. The just one dies unjustly for the unjust to make them just!

Pilate released Barabbas and ordered Jesus to be scourged.

The Scourging of Jesus

Jesus was then tied to a single post and then publicly scourged. The Romans did these things quite publicly for humiliation and as an object lesson to the remainder of the citizens.

It seems that the purpose of this brutal punishment was to bring a person that was to be crucified near to the point of death so that their time on the cross would not be long. Mel Gibson's movie shows the scourging very accurately, except that the Roman's removed all clothing from the victim and the movie was not nearly as brutal as it truly was.[1]

The whip used for scourging was called a flagellum and it had several leather straps with a metal ball, bone, glass, or whatever they could find that would cause damage. The whip would be applied with the full force of the Roman guard, the object at the end of the whip would embed in the flesh, and the whip would then be jerked away tearing off the flesh and then the muscles. It is hard to describe how truly brutal this was. It was entirely possible to scourge a victim to death, if desired. If the victim was to be crucified, the Centurion in charge would stop the scourging so that there could be a crucifixion. Remember that Jesus knew that he was to be scourged and accepted it for you and me.

Whipping Throughout the Bible – 1 Kings 12:11

When Rehoboam became king after Solomon's death, he said that, "[. . .] My father hath chastised you with whips, but I will chastise you with scorpions" (KJV, 1 Kings 12:11). The scorpions refer to putting hooks on the end of the strap which caused even more severe injury. Deuteronomy 25:3 specified that the victim must not receive more than forty lashes, so the custom was to limit the punishment to thirty-nine lashes. Paul referred to thirty-nine stripes in 2 Corinthians 11:24. The lash the Jews used was a single rod and did not cause the injury that a Roman flagellum did.

Soldiers Mock Jesus – Matt. 27:27–31, Mark 15:16–20, John 19:2–3

After they had publicly scourged Jesus, they returned his clothing and took him into the Praetorium (governor's palace). The entire governor's garrison (about 400–600) men gathered around to witness the *fun*. This time they took away his outer garments and gave him a scarlet robe and made a crown from a thorn-bush. The crown was pushed down on his head so that the thorns pierced the skin. A reed was placed in his right hand to simulate a scepter. The Romans used a strong reed to administer corporal punishment on errant soldiers. A likely variety of reed grows abundantly on the banks of the Jordan River and is often used as a walking stick. The soldiers then ridiculed Jesus by bowing down on a knee and saluted him with "Hail, King of the Jews" (Mark 15:18). They then spat on Jesus, slapped him, and using the reed, beat him on the head, forcing the thorns deeper into his head. Great sport!

Pilate's Final Appeal – John 19:4–6

Pilate went back to the Jews waiting outside his palace and said that he was bringing Jesus back outside and that he found no fault in him. Jesus was led out and Pilate (probably pointing to him) pronounced, "Behold the Man" (John 19:5). Pilate seems convinced that Jesus was not guilty of anything more than being a troublemaker to the Jews and crucifixion was not warranted. Jesus remained calm, meek, and patient throughout his ordeal.

The Jews' Response – John 19:7–8

The Jews responded, "We have a law, and according to our law He ought to die, because He made Himself the Son of God" (John 19:7). Blasphemy. They changed their accusation; their first accusation had been sedition. This is demonstrated in Luke 23:2, "And they began to accuse Him, saying, 'We found this fellow perverting the nation, and forbidding to pay taxes to Caesar, saying that He Himself is Christ, a King.'" When Pilate heard this, he was more afraid or concerned. He had several reasons to be concerned because He knew that Jesus was innocent, and he did not see justification for execution. Pilate also knew that the Jews were spiteful and full of hatred, but that did not justify execution. If he didn't do what they were yelling for, they might cause a rebellion, which he could not tolerate. Also, the Roman's worshipped many gods, and he was afraid of executing a god and the wrath of the gods for executing one of their own.

Pilate went back into his palace and confronted Jesus, asking "Where are you from" (John 19:9). Jesus did not answer, probably for a number of reasons. Jesus had already told Pilate of his design and the nature of his kingdom (John 18:36–37). Also, Jesus had already said enough to prove his innocence and Pilate was convinced of his innocence. It is also likely that Pilate would not have understood the truth of Jesus' origin. Lastly, Jesus knew that there was no expectation of justice. He knew what his mission was and that had to go to the cross for you and me.

In John 19:10–11, Pilate sounded frustrated by Jesus' silence. "Are You not speaking to me? Do you not know that I have power to crucify You, and power to release You" (John 19:10). Jesus corrected Pilate by telling him, "You could have no power at all against Me unless it had been given you from above. Therefore the one [Judas Iscariot, the high-priests, and the Sanhedrin] who delivered Me to you has the greater sin" (John 19:11).

Pilate Returns to the Crowd – John 19:12–13

Pilate went back before the Jews and tried to convince them that Jesus should be released. They answered Pilate, "If you let this Man go, you are not Caesar's friend. Whoever makes himself a king speaks against Caesar" (John 19:12). This was a direct threat to Pilate. The Roman emperor was Tiberius and was known to be cruel, jealous, and wicked. If the Jews made it known to Tiberius that Pilate was no friend of his, Pilate was a dead man. "When Pilate therefore heard that saying, he brought Jesus out and sat down in the judgment seat in a place that is called *The* Pavement, but in Hebrew, Gabbatha" (John 19:13).

The Crowd Calls for Jesus' Crucifixion – John 19:14

It was the preparation day for the Passover, that is daytime of the thirteenth of Nisan. Passover was a high holy day beginning at sundown, and as a high holy day, it was a sabbath day. John said that it was the sixth hour (noon). However, in Mark 15:25, Mark (Peter) said it was the third hour (9:00 a.m.). Pilate said to the Jews "Behold your King" (John 19:14).

"But they cried out, 'Away with Him, away with Him! Crucify Him!' Pilate said to them, 'Shall I crucify your King?' The chief priests answered, 'We have no king but Caesar'" (John 19:15).

> *For the children of Israel shall abide many days without king or prince, without sacrifice* [after 70 AD] *or sacred pillar, without ephod* [apron worn by high priest] *or teraphim* [figurine of household god]. *Afterward the children of Israel shall return and seek the Lord their God and David their king. They shall fear the Lord and His goodness in the latter days* (Hos. 3:4–5).

Pilate Washes His Hands – Matt. 27:24–25

Once Pilate realized that the crowd could not be moved, he called for a water dish to be brought out and he washed his hands, saying, "I am innocent of the blood of this just Person. You see to it" (Matt. 27:24). The crowd answered, "His blood *be* on us and on our children" (Matt. 27:25). This was a terrible choice, in less than forty years that curse would cost Israel the destruction of Jerusalem, their beloved temple, over a million deaths, and many taken into slavery. In John 19:16–17, Pilate turned Jesus over to the Jews to be crucified. They took Jesus to be crucified, "And He, bearing His cross, went out to a place called the Place of a Skull, which is called in Hebrew, Golgotha" (John 19:17).

CHAPTER TWENTY-ONE

JOURNEY TO GOLGOTHA: WEDNESDAY DAYTIME, THE THIRTEENTH OF NISAN

We typically are presented with pictures of Jesus carrying his entire cross. The entire cross would weigh several hundred pounds and after scourging, the victim would be unable to carry this weight. Several articles I've read suggest that the Romans set the upright post permanently and the victim carried his own patibulum or transverse beam of the cross to the execution site. It has been estimated that the transverse beam would weigh about a hundred pounds, a more manageable weight. Pick up a sack of concrete, which weighs ninety-six pounds. Not too bad?

Carrying the Cross – Matt. 27:32, Mark 15:21, Luke 23:26–32

Jesus was probably too weak to carry the cross himself and a by-stander, Simon of Cyrene was compelled to carry the cross for Jesus. Cyrene was a major North African center of Judaism and is located near the modern area of Tripoli. Luke writes that a great multitude of people followed him and the women mourned and lamented his crucifixion. Jesus told them not to mourn for him, rather they should mourn for themselves and their children. Jesus knew the coming destruction of Jerusalem and the terror that would be brought on them. Luke 23:31 says: "For if they do these things in the green wood, what will be done in the dry?" One meaning of this is, "if the Romans do this to me, who is innocent and blameless, what will they do to this guilty nation?" The procession to Calvary included two criminals that were to be put to death along with Jesus.

The King on a Cross – Matt. 27:33–36

They took Jesus to Golgotha, also known as the Place of a Skull. The Romans then offered Jesus some sour wine, mixed with myrrh. Myrrh was presented to Jesus by the wise men who visited him after his birth. Myrrh is often used as a perfume, but it can be processed and added to wine to be highly intoxicating. The suggestion has been made that they were offering Jesus something to reduce or deaden his pain. Jesus knew that he had to suffer the pain and penalty and he did not want to be denied suffering for us. The Romans then stripped him naked, nailed his wrists to the cross member, lifted him up, set him on the vertical beam, and then his feet were nailed to this beam.

King of the Jews – Matt. 27:37, Luke 23:38, John 19:19–22

When Pilate sent Jesus off to be crucified, he wrote on a plaque "Jesus of Nazareth, The King of the Jews" (John 19:19). He wrote this in Roman, Greek, and Hebrew. This plaque was carried before the guilty party and attached to the cross to show the citizens what this person had done to deserve this punishment. The priests did not like this writing and tried to get Pilate to change it, but he said, "What I have written, I have written" (John 19:22).

Anytime the priests get upset, pay attention. In Hebrew, if one takes the first letter of each phrase that was written, it spells YHWH, which is the unpronounceable name Of God. It could be that Pilate believed that Jesus was YHWH, or it could have been that Pilate wanted to make mischief with the Jews and to pay them back for what they had done to him.

The Romans Gamble of Jesus' Garments – Matt. 27:35–36, John 19:23–24

The Romans then shared his belongings, but his outer tunic was one piece and they choose to cast lots, or gamble, to see who got it. They remained with the crucified to ensure no one took them down without permission.

CHAPTER TWENTY-TWO

JESUS ON THE CROSS: WEDNESDAY DAYTIME, THE THIRTEENTH OF NISAN

The First Word – Luke 23:34

In verse 34 Jesus spoke, "Father, forgive them, for they do not know what they do". He saw that the soldiers who had just nailed him to the cross were casting lots over his clothes. It is likely that he thought of Caiaphas and the Sanhedrin, and their sin which the citizens of Jerusalem would pay for. Of the eleven remaining disciples, only John was standing by him, while the others had deserted him. Where were the crowds that called out "hosannas" when he entered Jerusalem a few days before? Could he also have been thinking of us, who daily forget him in our lives? Throughout his ministry, Jesus taught that we are to forgive. He was on the cross, paying the price that we all so richly deserve, and in love he asked his Father to forgive.

Jesus Blasphemed – Matt. 27:39–44, Mark 15:29–32, Luke 23:35–37

The people standing around the cross called to Jesus and challenged him to save himself if he was the King. They called out that if he would destroy the temple and rebuild it in three days, he could come down off the cross. The priests said, "He saved others; Himself He cannot save. If He is the King of Israel, let Him now come down from the cross, and we will believe Him" (Matt. 27:41–42). He would, just not the way they expected. He would die on the cross, be buried, and then resurrected. He would indeed come down off the cross, and they still did not believe.

The Second Word – Luke 23:39–43

One of the criminals said, "If you are the Christ, save Yourself and us" (Luke 23:39). This was not an appeal for forgiveness or salvation. He just wanted down off the cross. The other criminal answered him, "Do you not even fear God, seeing you are under the same condemnation? And we indeed justly, for we receive the due reward for our deeds; but this Man has done nothing wrong" (Luke 23:40–41). He then spoke to Jesus, "Lord, remember me when You come into Your kingdom" (Luke 23:42). Jesus replied, "Assuredly, I say to you, today you will be with Me in Paradise" (Luke 23:43). *Barnes' Notes on the New Testament* list four lessons.[1] The first is that the soul will exist separately from the body; for, while the thief and the Savior would be in Paradise, their bodies would be on the cross or in the grave. The second is that immediately after death (the same day) the souls of the righteous will be made happy. They will feel that they are secure; they will be received among the just; and they will have the assurance of a glorious immortality.

Third, the state will differ from the condition of the wicked. The promise was made to but one on the cross, and there is no evidence whatever that the other entered there. Also see the parable of the rich man and Lazarus (Luke 16:19–31). Lastly, it is the chief glory of this state and of heaven to be permitted to see Jesus Christ and to be with him.

> *So we are always confident, knowing that while we are at home in the body we are absent from the Lord. For we walk by faith, not by sight. We are confident, yes, well pleased rather to be absent from the body and to be present with the Lord* (2 Cor. 5:6–8).

The Third Word – Mark 15:40, John 19:25–27

"[. . .] He said to His Mother, 'Woman, behold your son!' Then He said to the disciple, 'Behold your mother'" (John 19:26–27). Even though Jesus was hanging on the cross, in indescribable and unimaginable pain and humiliation, his concern went out to others. He spent his ministry preaching love and compassion for others, and here he demonstrates it. There were several women standing nearby, Mary his mother, Mary of Cleopas (his mother's sister), Mary Magdalene, Mary the mother of James the Less and Joseph, Salome the mother of Zebedee's children (James and John). The only disciple mentioned is the one he loved, John. It is interesting that Jesus did not depend on James or his other siblings. It is suggested that this is proof that they were Joseph's children from a previous marriage, and not from the union of Joseph and Mary. Mark 6:3 further supports this suggestion when Jesus is called the "son of Mary", and not "one of the sons of Mary".

Darkness Over the Land – Matt. 27:45

From the sixth hour (noon) until the ninth hour (3:00 p.m.) there was darkness over all the land. Jesus died at the ninth hour, the same time the Passover lamb was being slain in the temple. This could not have been an eclipse of the sun, for the Passover was at the time of the full moon, when the moon is opposite to the sun. No explanation is given in the scriptures, it could have been a dust cloud, cloud of insects, or the hand of God.

The Fourth Word – Ps. 22, Matt. 27:46, Mark 15:34

In Matthew 27:46 Jesus cried, "My God, My God, why have You forsaken Me?" It is important to note that Jesus did not call out for his Father. He called out to "My God". I have had it explained that Jesus had become sin for us, and that God cannot abide with sin, so he departed from Jesus, and turned away so he did not watch his Son suffer this way. I can imagine the painful wail that Jesus made. He always had a very close relationship with his Father, but at this time his Father left him. This was far worse than suddenly, without warning, losing your beloved. My experience has been that it feels like someone barehanded reached into my chest and ripped out my heart. It is hard to imagine the dread, pain, emptiness, and total loss that Jesus felt.

The Fifth Word – John 19:28

In John 19:28 Jesus spoke, "I thirst." This is the only human expression of his suffering. It is understood that through the loss of body fluids, blood, sweat, and other bodily fluids, the victim becomes very thirsty. This fulfills the prophecy in Psalms 69:21, "And for my thirst they gave me vinegar to drink". John does not identify who provided the vinegar (sour wine), but this person used a hyssop branch and held a sponge to Jesus' lips for him to get a drink.

The Sixth Word – Matt. 27:50, John 19:29–30

In John 19:30, Jesus spoke, "It is finished". Jesus' mission on Earth has been successfully finished! All that was his to do, he did. Jesus had come to be the final and perfect sacrifice for our sins, and he completed his mission. The era of a blood sacrifice was over. Now we may approach God, seeking atonement for our sins, and we will be forgiven and accepted as a child of God.

The Seventh Word – Luke 23:46

In Luke 23:46, Jesus said, "Father, 'into Your hands I commit My spirit'". This is a quote from Psalms 31:5, "Into Your hand I commit my spirit; You have redeemed me, O Lord God of truth." Jesus said this with his head bowed and then he breathed his last.

For God so loved the world that He gave His only begotten Son, that whoever believes in Him should not perish but have everlasting life (John 3:16).

CHAPTER TWENTY-THREE

THE CRUCIFIXION FROM A SCIENTIFIC STANDPOINT

"Medical Aspects of the Crucifixion: The Agony of Love" by Dr. Mark Eastman[1] is an article which presents the events surrounding Jesus' crucifixion in medical terminology that is very explicit. The following is my commentary on Dr. Eastman's work. Remember that the cross was Jesus' goal in order that he might suffer so that we might have redemption. During the last evening, Jesus taught that "Greater love has no one than this, than to lay down one's life for his friends" (John 15:13). Jesus demonstrated this love on the cross and it seems reasonable that we should return to him our love.

Dr. Eastman notes that when Jesus prayed in the Garden of Gethsemane, great drops of blood fell to the ground. He gave it as his opinion that could have been a condition known as hematohidrosis which happens when capillary blood vessels that feed the sweat glands rupture, causing them to bleed as one would sweat, with great drops. The doctor explains that this may occur under conditions of extreme emotional stress. Jesus, being a man (and a God) and knowing the torture that he was going to endure, would be under extreme stress. He even said, "Father, if it is Your will, take this cup away from Me; nevertheless not My will, but Yours, be done" (Luke 22:42). Jesus knew what was going to happen, he didn't look forward to it, but he knew that it must be done so that we could be forgiven. I am so humbled that Jesus himself would endure what he did for you and me.

Dr. Eastman then notes that Jesus had not had anything to drink since the night before, so the combination of the beatings, the crown of thorns, and the scourging would have set into motion an irreversible process of severe dehydration and cardiorespiratory failure. All of this was done so that the prophecy of Isaiah would be fulfilled, "I gave My back to those who struck *Me*, And My cheeks to those who plucked out the beard; I did not hide My face from shame and spitting" (Isa. 50:6). Additionally, Isaiah 53:5 states, "But He *was* wounded for our transgressions, *He was* bruised for our iniquities; The chastisement for our peace *was* upon Him, And by His stripes we are healed".

Dr. Eastman explains that crucifixion was invented by the Persians between 300-400 BC. It was "perfected" by the Romans in the first century BC. It is arguably the most painful death ever invented by man and is where we get our term "excruciating". It was reserved primarily for the most vicious of criminals. The victim was then placed on his back, arms stretched out and nailed to the cross bar. The nails, which were generally about seven to nine inches long, were placed between the bones of the forearm (the radius and ulna) and the small bones of the hands (the carpal bones).

The placement of the nail at this point had several effects. First it ensured that the victim would indeed hang there until their death. Secondly, a nail placed at this point would sever the largest nerve in the hand called the median nerve.

The severing of this nerve is a medical catastrophe. In addition to severe burning pain the destruction of this nerve causes permanent paralysis of the hand. Furthermore, by nailing the victim at this point in the wrist, there would be minimal bleeding and there would be no bones broken! Thus, scriptures were fulfilled: "I can count all My bones. They look and stare at Me" (Ps. 22:17) and "He guards all his bones; Not one of them is broken" (Ps. 34:20).

The positioning of the feet is probably the most critical part of the mechanics of crucifixion. First the knees were flexed about forty-five degrees and the feet were flexed (bent downward) an additional forty-five degrees until they were parallel the vertical pole. An iron nail about seven to nine inches long was driven through the feet between the second and third metatarsal bones. In this position, the nail would sever the dorsal pedal artery of the foot, but the resultant bleeding would be insufficient to cause death. The resulting position on the cross set up a horrific sequence of events which resulted in a slow, painful death. Having been pinned to the cross, the victim then had an impossible position to maintain.

With the knees flexed at about forty-five degrees, the victim bore his weight with the muscles of the thigh. However, this was almost an impossible task; try to stand with your knees flexed at forty-five degrees for five minutes. As the strength of the legs gave out, the weight of the body had to be borne by the arms and shoulders. The result was that within a few minutes of being placed on the cross, the shoulders would become dislocated. Minutes later the elbows and wrists would become dislocated. The result of these dislocations was that the arms were as much as six to nine inches longer than normal.

With the arms dislocated, considerable body weight was transferred to the chest, causing the rib cage to be elevated in a state of perpetual inhalation. Consequently, in order to exhale, the victim had to push down on his feet to allow the rib muscles to relax. The problem was that the victim could not push very long because the legs were extremely fatigued. As time went on, the victim was less and less able to bear weight on the legs, causing further dislocation of the arms and further raising of the chest wall, making breathing more and more difficult.

The result of this process was a series of catastrophic physiological effects. Because the victim could not maintain adequate ventilation of the lungs, the blood oxygen level began to diminish and the blood carbon dioxide (CO_2) level began to rise. This rising CO_2 level stimulated the heart to beat faster to increase the delivery of oxygen and the removal of CO_2.

However, due to the pinning of the victim and the limitations of oxygen delivery, the victim could deliver more oxygen and the rising heart rate only increased the oxygen demand. This process set up a vicious cycle of increasing oxygen demand, which could not be met, followed by an ever-increasing heart rate. After several hours, the heart began to fail, the lungs collapsed and filled up with fluid, which further decreased oxygen delivery to the tissues. The blood loss and hyperventilation combined to cause severe dehydration. That's why Jesus said, "I thirst" (John 19:28).

Over a period of several hours, the combination of collapsing lungs, a failing heart, dehydration, and the inability to get adequate oxygen supplies to the tissues cause the eventual death of the victim. The victim, in effect, could not breathe properly and slowly suffocated to death. In cases of severe cardiac stress, such as crucifixion, a victim's heart could even burst. This process is called "cardiac rupture." Therefore, it could be said that Jesus died of a broken heart!

To slow the process of death, the executioners put a small wooden seat on the cross, which would allow the victim the privilege of bearing his weight on his buttocks. The effect of this was that it could take up to nine days to die on a cross.

When the Romans wanted to expedite death, they would simply break the legs of the victim, causing suffocation in a matter of minutes. At 3:00 p.m. in the afternoon, Jesus said, "Tetelastai," meaning "it is finished" (John 19:30). He then gave up his spirit. "Then the soldiers came and broke the legs of the first and of the other who was crucified with Him. But when they came to Jesus and saw that He was already dead, they did not break His legs" (John 19:32–33).

CHAPTER TWENTY-FOUR

SIGNS AT JESUS' DEATH: WEDNESDAY DAYTIME, THE THIRTEENTH OF NISAN

The Veil is Torn – Matt. 27:51–53

The veil of the temple was torn in two from the top to the bottom. The construction of the veil was given in Exodus 26:3–33, but it was a hand's breadth (four inches) thick, eighteen cubits (about thirty feet) tall, and very heavy. This happened while the priests were doing their daily sacrifice. It has been suggested that this represented God rending his holy garments at his Son's death. The veil's purpose was to separate the holy place from the Holy of Holies. The holy place was visited by the high priest daily to make sacrifice. However, the Holy of Holies was visited only once a year, on the Day of Atonement. The veil was also there to protect man from God, but with the death of Jesus, God became our friend and we no longer needed to be protected. Also, tearing the veil meant that the age of sacrifices had been ended. Jesus was the Passover Lamb and there was no longer any requirement for blood offerings.

Centurion Acknowledges the Son of God – Matt. 27:54, Mark 15:39

When the centurion and the Roman execution squad experienced the earthquake and opening of graves, they were very afraid and said, "Truly this was the Son of God" (Matt. 27:54). In an earlier version, the centurion said, "a son of a god"; an expression perfectly correct for someone who believed that there were many gods.[1]

Jesus' Side is Pierced – John 19:31–37

This was the Preparation Day, Wednesday after 3 p.m., the thirteenth of Nisan. Jewish law required that the bodies should not remain on the cross after sundown because sundown was the start of the high sabbath; the high holy days of the Feast of the Unleavened Bread. No work could be done on the high sabbath, so the bodies must be taken down off the cross and disposed of before sundown. Death on the cross is usually quite slow and could take days of agony. The Jews had arranged with Pilate that their legs should be broken to expedite their death. This was done to the two criminals, but when they Roman guards got to Jesus, they determined that he was already dead. To ensure that Jesus was dead, one of them took a spear and impaled him in the side, up to his heart. This fulfilled two prophecies: "Not one of His bones shall be broken" (Ex. 12:46, Num. 9:12, Ps. 34:20) and "They shall look on him whom they pierced" (Zech. 12:10).

Jesus is Buried – Matt. 27:57–61, Mark 15:42–47, John 19:38–42, Luke 23:50–56

After the execution was completed, a follower of Jesus named Joseph of Arimathea went to Pilate and asked for the body of Jesus. John 19:38 said that Joseph was secretly a follower of Jesus. He had kept his devotion a secret because of his fear of the Jews. Luke reports that he was "a council member, a good and just man" (Luke 23:50). Gill calls him an honorable counselor.[2] A counselor was a member of the Sanhedrin, one who sat in the chamber of the counselors in the high priest's chamber. The location of Arimathea is not documented other than it was a city of Jews. It is usually identified with either Ramleh or Ramathaim-Zophim, where David came to Samuel (1 Sam. 19).

The Romans preferred to leave the body on the cross to rot to continue the lesson to the citizens and to say, "don't mess with us". However, Jewish custom would not permit this and required the bodies be removed from the cross before sundown. Pilate was surprised that Jesus was already dead and sent for the Centurion to verify his death. The Centurion reported to Pilate that Jesus was dead and Pilate gave permission for Joseph to take the body.

Nicodemus (John 3) purchased a mixture of myrrh and aloes, about a hundred pounds of weight. Remember that myrrh was presented to Jesus by the wise men when Jesus was an infant. Myrrh was an expensive yellowish-brown, sweet smelling gum resin that was obtained from a tree and had a bitter taste. It was chiefly used as a chemical for embalming the dead. Aloe was a sweet-smelling fragrance derived from the juices pressed from the leaves of a tree. It was used to ceremonially cleanse, purify, and counteract the terrible smell of the corpse as it decomposed. Like myrrh, this substance was also very expensive and rare.

They took the body, cleaned it, covered it in the myrrh and aloes, and wrapped it in high a quality linen cloth. As far as Joseph and Nicodemus knew, this was the end of Jesus and they were going to honor him and take care of his body the best way they could. Joseph and Nicodemus placed Jesus' body in Joseph's tomb and rolled a large rock over the entrance. Mary Magdalene and Mary, the mother of James the Less and Joseph, sat near the tomb. There is no mention of Jesus' mother or John (Mark 15:40).

CHAPTER TWENTY-FIVE

PILATE ORDERS A GUARD SET: WEDNESDAY NIGHT TO DAWN THURSDAY, THE FOURTEENTH OF NISAN

Jesus was in the grave the first night. This was the time where the head of the family was to eat the Passover meal and be with his family. It is the first day of the Feast of the Unleavened Bread, the high holy day of the Jewish calendar.

Guarding Jesus' Body – Matthew 27:62

It is possible that the chief priests and Pharisees met while Jesus was on the cross and agreed to set a guard at his tomb. It is then possible that after sundown, before they went to their homes for the Passover meal, they met with Pilate. They were concerned that Jesus' disciples would use the cover of darkness to steal his body and claim resurrection. In Matthew 12:40 Jesus said that he would be in the heart of the earth for three days and three nights. Specifying days and nights nullify the argument that Jesus would be in the grave two night periods and one day period.

The Pharisees' Concerns – Matt. 27:63

The Pharisees called Jesus the deceiver, furthering their belief that Jesus deceived the people when he was alive by saying that he was the Son of God. This is what they called him during the trials, and they continued their argument. They knew that Pilate had a favorable opinion of Jesus, and they were maintaining a consistent argument. The phrase "while he was still alive" (Matt. 27:63) proves that they knew Jesus was dead, and they were concerned that there would be a great uproar if the people believed that he had, in fact, been resurrected and actually was the Son of God. Avoiding uproar was one of the Pharisees concerns, another was that they had to be right and avoid the charge that they crucified their Messiah.

Pharisee Request – Matt. 27:64

The Pharisees requested that Pilate set a guard and seal the tomb to prevent the reports of Jesus' disappearance being connected to his resurrection. In their minds, the first deception was when Jesus said that he was the Son of God. The second would have been if the disciples stole the body and proclaimed that Jesus had risen. The Pharisees needed to destroy the *myth* that Jesus was the Son of God and preserve their status as the leaders of Judaism.

Pilate Responds – Matt. 27:65–66

Pilate's response is very special, "You have a guard; go your way, make *it* as secure as you know how" (Matt. 27:65). I believe that Pilate accepted that Jesus was the Son of God and the Pharisees could do nothing to keep Jesus in the grave. When Pilate said, "make *it* as secure as you know how" (Matt. 27:65), there is a degree of contempt in his statement. He could almost have added "good luck". The Pharisees did set a guard, and put a seal on the grave, likely a wax seal, so that the grave could not be tampered with without leaving evidence. To the Romans, a guard consisted of about sixty men with a Centurion in charge.

Thursday Daytime, the Fourteenth of Nisan

This was the high sabbath day and there are no events reported. Jesus was in the grave the first day.

Thursday Night to Dawn Friday, the Fifteenth of Nisan

There were no events reported. Jesus was in the grave the second night.

Friday Daytime, the Fifteenth of Nisan

Jesus was in the grave the second day. Mary Magdalene, Mary the mother of James the Less, and Salome the mother of James and John purchased spices to anoint Jesus (Mark 16:1). They were apparently not aware that this had already been done by Joseph of Arimathea and Nicodemus. Where Joseph and Nicodemus could afford to purchase prepared spices, the women likely purchased the raw ingredients and had to cook them down to make them ready for the corpse. It is also possible that they purchased sweet smelling spices to adorn the sepulcher. In any case, resurrection was not expected.

Friday Night to Dawn Saturday, the Sixteenth of Nisan

This was the weekly sabbath and no activities were reported. Jesus was in the grave the third night.

Saturday Daytime, the Sixteenth of Nisan

This was the weekly sabbath and no activities were reported. Jesus was in the grave the third day.

CHAPTER TWENTY-SIX

THREE DAYS AND THREE NIGHTS: SATURDAY NIGHT TO DAWN SUNDAY, THE SEVENTEENTH OF NISAN

The events that follow have been put in the following order to the best of my ability in discerning their sequence. The persons involved are all moving at the same time in different directions, so complete accuracy cannot be assured.

The Stone is Moved – Matt. 28:1–4, Mark 16:1–4, Luke 24:1–5, John 20:1

Sometime during this period, Jesus was resurrected. All four gospels agree that Mary Magdalene and the other women who were at the cross went to the grave before the sun had risen. Consider their love and devotion; they had left the safety of the city during the night, without a man, to visit Jesus' grave. Safety concerns aside, going out of the city at night without a man for protection was just not done by women of that age.

As they approached the tomb, they discussed among themselves how they would roll the stone away from the tomb. When they arrived at the tomb, the found the stone rolled away. The two guards looked as though they were dead, likely they were unconscious. There was an angel near the opening to the tomb. He is described with a countenance like lightning (luster and brightness) and clothing like snow. Standing guard duty between midnight and dawn is a horrible watch, I've done it a few times. Having two angels of God suddenly appear would be a shock, even to a veteran Roman soldier who had seen many horrible things in battle and was fearless of danger. It is also possible that the angels rendered them unconscious.

I am quite sure that the stone was not removed so that Jesus could exit the tomb. Rather the stone was removed so that the women and disciples could see for themselves that Jesus was gone.

Mary Magdalene Runs for Peter and John – John 20:2–3

Mary Magdalene led the women into the tomb, and when she saw that the stone had been moved, it seems that she immediately turned and left without ever entering the tomb. She ran to Peter and John, and when she arrived she said, "They have taken away the Lord out of the tomb, and we do not know where they have laid Him" (John 20:2). The three of them leave for the tomb.

Women Enter the Tomb – Matt. 28:5–8, Mark 16:5–8, Luke 24:4–10

After Mary left to get Peter and John, the remaining women entered the tomb and saw two angels standing at the right and left side of the crypt where Jesus had been laid. The women were very afraid and bowed down on so that their faces were on the ground. An angel said to the remaining women, "Why do you seek the living among the dead" (Luke 24:5). The angels explained that Jesus was not dead, and asked, "Why are you looking for Him here?" Jesus also does not live in dead sinners or lifeless teachers, but among his church family. The angel continued, telling them to remember what Jesus had taught (Matt. 16:21, Mark 8:31, Luke 9:22), that he will be delivered into the hands of sinful men, crucified, and be raised on the third day. The women remembered what Jesus had taught and knew that he had been resurrected. The angel told them to tell the disciples and Peter. By specifying Peter, the angel was assuring him that his denials had been forgiven and that he was welcome. They left the tomb with great joy and ran to the disciples.

Women Meet Jesus – Matthew 28:9–10

On their way to the disciples, the women were stopped by Jesus who said, "Rejoice" (Matt. 28:9). This was a common phrase used by Jesus. The women recognized him as Jesus resurrected, thus confirming what the angel had told them in the tomb. The women fell down and held him by his feet and worshipped him. Being able to grasp his feet confirmed that he was physical, not a spirit. Jesus said to them, "Do not afraid. Go *and* tell My brethren to go to Galilee, and there they will see me" (Matt. 28:10). This is first time Jesus used the word brethren to describe his disciples.

Somehow these women did not meet with Peter, John, and Mary Magdalene who were heading toward the tomb. The women followed Jesus' instructions and continued on to the disciples. They told them the good news that Jesus was alive, but the disciples did not believe, they considered it idle talk. This supports the idea that the resurrection was not expected and not planned by the disciples. The resurrection was a shock and was not believed until that night when Jesus appeared in their midst.

Peter and John Enter the Tomb – John 20:4–10

Peter and John ran back to the tomb, and Mary followed them. John, being the younger man, arrived first. He looked in and saw the linen cloths lying there, yet he did not go in. Peter arrived and went right into the tomb. Peter saw the linen cloths lying where the body was placed, and the handkerchief that had been placed over Jesus' face was folded neatly and placed to the side. John then entered the tomb, saw the linen wrapping and the handkerchief, "and believed" (John 20:8) Mary's report that Jesus' body was missing. They did not understand what had occurred, "For as yet they did not know the Scripture, that He must rise again from the dead" (John 20:9). Peter and John then returned to their own homes.

According to Gill, the handkerchief could be translated to "the girdle, or binding of the head", meaning not just a cloth laying over the face, but an object that was fastened to the head to cover the face and keep the mouth closed.[1] The evidence left behind shows clearly that there was no haste in removing the body. Jesus was brought back to life, he materialized outside of the burial cloths, and they collapsed where they were. The handkerchief was folded and placed nearby. Robbers would not have spent time removing the burial cloth; they would have grabbed the body and ran. The Roman guards were close by and would not have been too friendly with grave robbers.

Mary Magdalene Sees the Risen Lord – John 20:11–18

Mary followed Peter and John and when she arrived at the tomb, she stood outside crying. While crying and weeping, she looked into the tomb and saw the two angels sitting at the head and foot of the crypt where Jesus had been. They ask her why she was crying and she said that someone had taken her Lord and she did not know where they had placed his body. It seems that she thought that Joseph of Arimathea had moved the body to a more permanent location. It is likely that the angels saw Jesus standing behind her and they were struck with awe and reverence. She turned around and Jesus was standing behind her, but she did not recognize that it was him. Instead, she presumed that it was Joseph's gardener. Jesus asked why she was weeping and who she was looking for. Mary, continuing her belief that Joseph or the gardener had moved the body, asked for the location so that she could take it away.

Jesus said, "Mary!" (John 20:16) and her eyes were opened and saw that it was Jesus. She called him "Rabboni" (John 20:16), which means "Lord of the world", expressing her faith in his power as part of the Godhead.[2] It seems that she tried to take hold of him and hang on; she did not want him to get away from her again. Jesus told her not to hang onto him; rather he wanted her to go to the disciples and share the great news. Mary followed his instructions and went to the disciples and reported that had happened and what Jesus had said.

CHAPTER TWENTY-SEVEN

SUNDAY DAYTIME, THE SEVENTEENTH OF NISAN

The Guards are Bribed – Matt. 28:11–15

Remember what Pilate said to the Jews "make it as secure as you know how" (Matt. 27:65)? It was a death penalty for a guard to sleep when he was on duty. When the women left the tomb, some of the guards went to Jerusalem and reported to the Sanhedrin that the tomb had been opened and the body was gone. The Sanhedrin decided that the best tactic was to say that while the guards were asleep the disciples stole the body and then lied that he had been resurrected. There are many problems with this lie. If the guards were asleep how did they know it was the disciples that took the body? How was it that moving the stone did not wake them?

If the body was stolen, why was the burial clothing left behind? If the guards woke up in time to see the disciples running away with the body, why didn't they pursue them? Why didn't they arrest the women and interrogate them? Was the entire guard force asleep, all sixty of them?

The Sanhedrin must have known the truth, and needed a lie to cover it up. The Sanhedrin gave the guards a large amount of money and promised them that they would protect them from Roman justice if word got back to Pilate that they had been sleeping on duty. This lie was spread by messenger throughout Israel and abroad. If a lie is repeated often enough and long enough, it becomes believed as truth. A classic example is the lie that Christ was crucified on Good Friday.

CHAPTER TWENTY-EIGHT

THE ROAD TO EMMAUS: SUNDAY AFTERNOON, THE SEVENTEENTH OF NISAN

Jesus Walks with His Followers – Mark 16:12–13, Luke 24:13–27, 1 Cor. 15:5

Two of Jesus' disciples, not of the eleven apostles, but of the disciples that followed Jesus, were walking back to Emmaus on the day of resurrection. One was Cleopas and the other is believed to be Luke. The true location of Emmaus is not known, but it is suspected that Emmaus is near the ruins called el Kubieheh which is about seven and half miles northwest of Jerusalem.

They were discussing the events of the Passover, Jesus' arrest, trials, crucifixion, burial, and the women's report that he had risen. While these two were walking on the road, sadly discussing the events of the last few days, Jesus came alongside them and walked with them. His true identity was hidden from the men for some time. Jesus asked what they were talking about and why they were so sad. Cleopas might as well have said, "What rock have you been living under that you don't know what has been going on in Jerusalem in the last few days?" Jesus said, "What things" (Luke 24:19).

Cleopas gave Jesus a brief history of the events of the past week and how Jesus was to save Israel from the Romans and set up a government. Cleopas then told how the women had gone to the tomb, found it empty, and how the angels proclaimed that Jesus was alive. He continued by saying that certain members of their group went to the tomb and found it empty as the women had said, but they did not see Jesus.

Jesus then called them, "O foolish ones, and slow of heart to believe in all that the prophets have spoken" (Luke 24:25). Jesus chastised them for their lack of understanding concerning the prophecies about Jesus' sufferings and resurrection. Jesus then proceeded to give these two a Bible study in the Scripture's predictions concerning himself. What an experience these two had, having the author explain what he had written!

The Disciples' Eyes Opened – Luke 24:28–35

As they came near Emmaus, Jesus said that he was going further, but the disciples encouraged him to spend the evening with them, as the day was nearly spent. Jesus joined the other two at one of their homes and they sat to enjoy a meal. Jesus, the stranger and a guest (not the host), blessed the food and broke the bread. When Jesus broke the bread the two disciples then understood who they had been walking and talking with. Jesus then vanished from their sight! Jesus had lived with them, taught them, crucified, died, buried, and then he was walking and talking with them. He is risen; he lives! Praise God! They shared with each other how their hearts had been lifted and how they were moved by Jesus' teaching. They immediately returned to Jerusalem to share their wonderful news. Luke did not say that they ran back, but I am sure they did more than stroll. They got back with the others and shared their good news, and the two from Emmaus were told by the apostles that Peter had seen Jesus also (Luke 24:34). Peter, who had denied Jesus three times, was given the grace to be the first apostle to see him. Jesus was no spirit or hallucination of the women, he had risen from the grave.

CHAPTER TWENTY-NINE

JESUS APPEARS TO HIS DISCIPLES: SUNDAY NIGHT TO DAWN MONDAY, THE EIGHTEENTH OF NISAN

Jesus Appears to the Disciples – Mark 16:14, Luke 24:36–43, John 20:19–25

While the assembled apostles, the two from Emmaus, the women, and others were talking about Jesus' resurrection, he materialized in the room. The doors had been shut and bolted for fear of the Jews; they were being charged with stealing the body and were being hunted. Jesus said, "Peace to you" (Luke 24:36). Imagine the jaw dropping shock, Jesus just did something that had never been done in recorded history by materializing in a secure, closed room. Everyone was in shock, terrified, and frightened! They assumed he was a spirit (ghost) or something like that. Jesus said, "Why are you troubled? And why do doubts arise in your hearts" (Luke 24:38). He had them touch his hands, side, and body and they accepted that this was not a spirit, but their resurrected Lord. He requested something to eat and they gave him some fish and a piece of honey comb. His eating proved that he was not a spirit.

Jesus repeated, "Peace to you! As the Father has sent Me, I also send you" (John 20:21). Jesus declared that they were commissioned to be ministers of his. He then breathed on the apostles and said, "Receive the Holy Spirit" (John 20:22). When man was created, God breathed into him the breath of life (Genesis 2:7). His breathing on them was a pledge that they would receive the Holy Spirit after he departed, on the day of Pentecost.[1]

Much ink has been spilled over John 20:23. According to Gill, only God can forgive sins, and Christ being God, has a power to do so likewise; but he never communicated any such power to his apostles. Gill continues by saying that for a man to assume the authority to forgive sins is the mark of the antichrist. Sins can only be forgiven through the blood of Christ, according to the riches of God's grace.[2]

Thomas was not present at this event, but when the disciples saw him, they said that they had seen the Lord. Thomas said, "Unless I see in His hands the print of the nails, and put my finger into the print of the nails, and put my hand into His side, I will not believe" (John 20:25).

SUNDAY NIGHT TO DAWN MONDAY, THE TWENTY-FIFTH OF NISAN

Seeing and Believing – John 20:26–29

This is the next Sunday night, seven days since their last meeting. From this it appears that the apostles had set this day (Sunday) as their sabbath, and it has been observed as such since. While they were meeting, Jesus materialized again and gave Thomas the opportunity to experience this miracle. Jesus again said, "Peace to you" (John 20:26) and Jesus directs Thomas to put his finger in the nail holes and into the hole made by the spear. He then directs Thomas, "Do not be unbelieving, but believing" (John 20:27). Thomas examined Jesus and said, "My Lord and my God" (John 20:28).

This has been considered clear proof of the divinity of Christ for the several reasons.[3] There is no evidence that this was a mere expression of surprise or astonishment. Thomas said this to Jesus, "Thomas [. . .] said unto Him" (John 20:28). Jesus did not correct Thomas and no pious man would have allowed such language to be addressed to him (Rev. 22:8–9). Jesus then commended Thomas for believing. Finally, if Thomas did not mean what he said, then it would have been profanity, and Jesus would not have commended him.

Jesus acknowledged that after Thomas had seen him, Thomas then believed. Jesus then said, "Blessed *are* those who have not seen and *yet* have believed" (John 20:29) Thomas is typically called doubting Thomas, but remember that none of the disciples believed Jesus was resurrected until they saw him and touched him. Also, until their minds were opened, none of the disciples understood Jesus' true mission. They all were looking for Jesus to throw off the Roman yoke and set up an earthly kingdom.

That You May Believe – John 20:30–31

John seemed to close his gospel by saying that there were many other things to write about, but he was led to write more. Enough had been written to establish that Jesus was God, and that believing, we may have eternal life.

Meeting at the Sea of Galilee, Unknown Date – John 21:1–14

A portion of the disciples were gathered; verse 2 lists those present as Peter, Thomas, Nathanael, the sons of Zebedee, and two others. John does not specify where the disciples were gathered, but in Mark 14:28 Jesus said, "But after I have been raised, I will go before you to Galilee." It is likely that they were there waiting for him. Peter said that he was going fishing and the others said they were going to join him. When Jesus was alive, benefactors provided for their necessities, but after the crucifixion the disciples were are on their own and needed to eat. Peter was a fisherman by trade, so going fishing was a natural thing for him. The others followed him and they all went out onto the lake.

They fished all night and caught nothing. Peter, a fisherman by trade, could not catch a single fish. Jesus was standing on the shore, but no one recognized him. He asked them if they had any food, and they told him they did not. Jesus then called out for them to cast their nets on the other side of the ship. They did and caught a multitude of fish, so much for our human skills and experience. Without Jesus we can do nothing, and when we obey him the harvest is incredible. This was the same event that happened when Jesus recruited Peter to be one of his disciples. It seems that this triggered an old memory in John and he recognized Jesus and he told Peter who it was. Peter put his outer clothes back on, jumped into the water, and swam to shore. The other disciples stayed with the boat and headed the hundred yards back to shore. When they arrived at shore, they found Jesus tending a fire, cooking fish and bread.

Jesus told them to bring some of their fish, and Peter went out into the lake and pulled the net in. They counted 153 large fish, and John mentioned that the net did not break. Jesus invited the disciples to eat some breakfast. John mentioned that this was the third time Jesus manifested himself to the disciples after the resurrection.

Jesus Questions Peter – John 21:15–17

The analysis of these three verses was taken from the IVP New Testament Commentary Series. [3,4] Jesus questioned Peter using his birth name, Simon, son of Jonah. Jesus changed his name to Peter when he became a disciple. Simon was a fisherman from Galilee, Peter was a fisher of men. Jesus was asking Peter if he loved him more than being a fisherman from Galilee. The Greek word for love in this verse is 'agapao' which means much beloved. Peter affirmed that he loved Jesus more than being a fisherman. The Greek translation for Peter's response was 'phileo' which means to be a friend or have affection. Jesus then said, "Feed My lambs" (John 21:15). The Greek translation of the word 'feed' is to provide nutrition for the flock. By specifying lambs, Jesus was referring to the most tender part of the flock, his little children. There is no greater evidence of one's love for Christ than to take care of these new, tender lambs of his.

Jesus asked Peter a second time if he loved Jesus (agapao, much beloved), and again Peter responded that he loves (phileo, friend) Jesus. This time Jesus said that Peter should "Tend My sheep" (John 21:16). The Greek here means to provide care, guidance, and protection which a shepherd provides for his flock.

For a third time, Jesus asked Peter if he loved Jesus. The final time Jesus used the same word for love that Peter had (phileo, friend). Repeating the question three times reminded Peter of the three times he had denied Jesus. Peter responded sadly, "Lord, You know all things; You know that I love you" (John 21:17). Peter continued with the use of phileo (friend). After Peter's denial, he had been humbled and would claim nothing greater than being a friend of Jesus. A person that has agapao love is someone who can be trusted to stand by his friend. A person that has phileo love is someone who may stand by his friend. Jesus responded, "Feed My sheep" (John 21:17), instructions that combined provision of nutrition and protection for the flock.

Jesus tells Peter About His Future – John 21:18–19

In John 21:18, Jesus said to Peter using words that convey considerable importance, "Most assuredly" (New King James), or "Verily, verily" (King James) depending on the version. He said to Peter that when he was younger, he dressed himself and went where he wanted. However, when Peter got older, he would hold out his hands and others would bind him, and take him places that he did not want to go. Jesus was telling Peter that the freedom he was enjoying would be taken from him and that he would die a martyr's death. John wrote this after Peter's death and knew how he was killed and that his death would glorify God. Jesus instructed Peter to follow him.

Peter Asks About John – John 21:20–22

Peter asked Jesus about his close friend, John. Peter wanted to know about how John would die. Jesus responded with "If I will that he remain till I come, what is that to you? You follow Me" (John 21:22). Jesus told Peter that John's future did not matter, Peter was to follow Jesus.

Meeting at a Mountain in Galilee, Unknown Date – Matt 28:7–10

While at the tomb, Jesus told the women to tell the brethren to meet him in Galilee. The specific place or time was not discussed, but it seems that everyone understood or they were led by the Holy Spirit.

The People Gather, Unknown Date – Matt. 28:16–17, Mark 15–18

Matthew specifies that the eleven disciples went to the mountain, but it seems that other disciples, including women were present. In 1 Corinthians 15:6, Paul said that five hundred people were present. I suspect that when the word got out that Jesus was going to be present, all of his followers went to the mountain. When Jesus made himself visible, most believed and worshipped him as the Messiah, but some still doubted as had some of his disciples in the Upper Room until they interacted with him.

The Great Commission, Unknown Date – Matt. 28:18–20, Mark 16:15–18

Jesus is the Son of God, and God put him in charge. Jesus said that all authority had been given to him in heaven and on earth. Jesus told his disciples (and us) to go throughout the entire world and preach the good news (gospel), making others into disciples, and baptize them in the name of the Father, and of the Son, and of the Holy Spirit. Jesus said those that believe that Jesus is Lord and accept him as the master of their life will be saved. The commission also says that we are to be baptized to publicly signify that we accept that we are sinners and that through baptism we publicly reject (die to) our previous life. Rejecting baptism endangers one's eternal interest by being ashamed of Christ before men (Mark 8:38).

Final Meeting in Jerusalem, Jesus Appears to His Brother, Unknown Date – 1 Cor. 15:7

There is only one verse about this visit by Paul, and James does not discuss it at all.

Jesus' Last Appearance to the Disciples, Date Unknown– Acts 1:4–8, Luke 24:44–49

In Acts, Luke said that for a period of forty days Jesus met with the apostles many times and he spoke of the kingdom of God. This means that there was quite a bit of material that was not included in the Gospels. The apostles pressed Jesus one last time when he was going to establish his earthly kingdom. Jesus responded, "It is not for you to know the times or seasons which the Father has put in His own authority" (Acts 1:7). It would take the Holy Spirit's intervention to get the apostles to understand the nature of his kingdom. Jesus opened their understanding on Jesus' time and again reviewed his mission and what they were to do, go unto all of the world and be his witnesses. This is our mission even today. Jesus had already taught them about the Holy Spirit (Comforter), and how he would be with them always. Here Jesus told them that soon they would be baptized with the Holy Spirit and that they were not to leave Jerusalem until they received the baptism. It turned out that in ten days, on the day of Pentecost, they received him and truly understood Jesus' kingdom.

Jesus' Ascension to Heaven, Unknown Date – Mark 16:19–20, Luke 24:50–53, Acts 1:9–12

After their meeting in Jerusalem, Jesus led the disciples to the Mount of Olives, one of his favorite places to retire. Jesus raised his hands, blessed his disciples with scriptural understanding and forgiving grace, and was raised up into a cloud in full daylight, with the disciples as witnesses that he ascended into heaven. Doing this in full daylight, in front of many witnesses gave them the ability to jointly testify that they had seen Jesus ascend into heaven.

There are three reasons for Jesus to ascend into heaven, his earthly duties on earth were complete, he needed to depart so that the Holy Spirit could come, he still has duties to perform in heaven. Jesus is our High Priest and he will perform the work of intercession on our behalf. Jesus will assume the duties of King of all creation.

The disciples stood, staring at the clouds that had received him. Two angels appeared next to them and asked, "Men of Galilee, why do you stand gazing up into heaven? This *same* Jesus, who was taken up from you into heaven, will so come in like manner as you saw Him go into heaven" (Acts 1:11).

Amen!

BIBLIOGRAPHY

INTRODUCTION:
1. "Eusebius, Life of Constantine, Book III, Chapter XVIII", Eusebius Pamphilus, accessed March 1, 2017, www.newadvent.org/fathers/25023.htm.
2. "The Ecclesiastical History of Theodoret, Book I, Chapter IX", Jerome Theodoret, accessed March 1, 2017, www.ccel.org/ccel/shaff/npnf203.iv.viii.i.x.html.
3. "Easter", Kaufmann Kohler, Jewish Encyclopedia, 1902, accessed March 1, 2017, www.jewishencyclopedia.com/articles/5399-easter.

CHAPTER THREE:
1. Hayyim Shauss, *Guide to Jewish Holy Days: History and Observance*, Schocken Books, 1938.

CHAPTER FIVE:
2. Sir Robert Anderson, "The Coming Prince", *Cosimo Inc.* (2007): 128.
3. "Bethany (biblical village)", Wikipedia, accessed March 1, 2017, https://en.wikipedia.org/wiki/Bethany_(biblical_village).

CHAPTER 7:
1. John Gill, *John Gill's Exposition of the Bible*, Tecarta Inc., Matthew 21:19.
2. John Gill, *John Gill's Exposition of the Bible*, Tecarta Inc., Matthew 22:11.
3. John Gill, *John Gill's Exposition of the Bible*, Tecarta Inc., Matthew 21:12.

CHAPTER 8:
1. Merriam-Webster, *Webster's Ninth New Collegiate Dictionary*, (Easton, 1985), 344.
2. Flavius Josephus, "War of the Jews, Book 5, Chapter 10, para 5", accessed March 1, 2017, www.biblestudytools.com.
3. John Gill, *John Gill's Exposition of the Bible*, Tecarta Inc., Matthew 25:1.

CHAPTER 9:
1. Flavius Josephus, "War of the Jews, Book 6, Chapter 9, para 3", accessed March 1, 2017 www.biblestudytools.com.

CHAPTER 11:
1. John Gill, *John Gill's Exposition of the Bible*, Tecarta Inc., John 13:10.
2. Lonnie Lane, "What if Wasn't a Rooster", Messianic Vision, accessed March 1, 2017, www.sidroth/articles/what-if-it-wasnt-rooster/.
3. John Gill, *John Gill's Exposition of the Bible*, Tecarta Inc., Luke:22:38.

CHAPTER 12:
1. Flavius Josephus, "Antiquities of the Jews, Book 15, Chapter 11, para 3", accessed March 1, 2017, www.biblestudytools.com/history/flavius-josephus/antiquities-jews.

CHAPTER 14:
1. Frederick Graves, "The Trial of Jesus", accessed March 1, 2017, www.jurisdictionary.com.

CHAPTER 17:
1. John Gill, John Gill's Exposition of the Bible, Tecarta Inc., Luke 22:66.
2. Flavius Josephus, "Wars of the Jews, Book 2, Chapter 8", accessed March 1, 2017, www.biblestudytools.com/history/flavius-josephus/war-of-the-jews.
3. Augustin Lémann, *Jesus Before the Sanhedrin*, trans. Julius Magath, (Palala Press: 2015).

CHAPTER 18:
1. Flavius Josephus, "Antiquities of the Jews, Book 18, Chapter 4, para 1&2", accessed March 1, 2017, www.biblestudytools.com/history/flavius-josephus/antiquities-jews.

CHAPTER 20:
1. Eusebius, "Eusebius' Ecclesiastical History, Book 4, Chapter 11", accessed March 1,

2017, www.ncbible.info/MoodRes/History/EusebiusChurchHistory.pdf.

CHAPTER 22:
1. Albert Barnes, *Barnes' Notes on the New Testament*, accessed March 1,2017 www.classic.studylight.org/com/bnn/view.cgi?book=lu.

CHAPTER 23:
1. Mark Eastman, "Medical Aspects of The Crucifixion: The Agony of Love", *Personal Update News Journal*, April 1998, accessed March 1, 2017, http://www.khouse.org/articles/1998/113/.

CHAPTER 24:
1. Albert Barnes, *Barnes' Notes on the New Testament*, accessed March 1, 2017, www.classic.studylight.org/com/bnn/view.cgi?book=mt&chapter=27.
2. John Gill, *John Gill's Exposition of the Bible*, Tecarta Inc., Luke 23:50.

CHAPTER 26:
1. John Gill, *John Gill's Exposition of the Bible*, Tecarta Inc., John 20:7.
2. John Gill, *John Gill's Exposition of the Bible*, Tecarta Inc., John 20:16.

CHAPTER 29:
1. John Gill, *John Gill's Exposition of the Bible*, Tecarta Inc., John 20:22.

2 John Gill, *John Gill's Exposition of the Bible*, Tecarta Inc., John 20:23.
3 Albert Barnes, *Barnes' Notes on the New Testament*, accessed March 1, 2017, www.classic.studylight.org/com/bnn/view.cgi?book=joh&chapter=20.
4 Grant R. Osborne, Ed., "The IVP New Testament Commentary Series", InterVarsity Press, accessed March 1, 2017, https://www.biblegateway.com/resources/ivp-nt/jesus-forms-peter-as-leader-as-disciple.

 WORLD AHEAD *press*

Self-publishing means that you have the freedom to blaze your own trail as an author. But that doesn't mean you should go it alone. By choosing to publish with WORLD AHEAD PRESS, you partner with WND—one of the most powerful and influential brands on the Internet.

If you liked this book and want to publish your own, WORLD AHEAD PRESS, co-publishing division of WND Books, is right for you. WORLD AHEAD PRESS will turn your manuscript into a high-quality book and then promote it through its broad reach into conservative and Christian markets worldwide.

IMAGINE YOUR BOOK ALONGSIDE THESE AUTHORS!

We transform your manuscript into a marketable book. Here's what you get:

BEAUTIFUL CUSTOM BOOK COVER
PROFESSIONAL COPYEDIT
INTERIOR FORMATTING
EBOOK CONVERSION
KINDLE EBOOK EDITION
WORLDWIDE BOOKSTORE DISTRIBUTION
MARKETING ON AMAZON.COM

It's time to publish your book with WORLD AHEAD PRESS.

Go to www.worldaheadpress.com for a Free Consultation

www.ingramcontent.com/pod-product-compliance
Lightning Source LLC
LaVergne TN
LVHW011203080426
835508LV00007B/563